职业教育汽车类专业"十三五"创新教材

U0367426

汽车专业英语　第3版

（彩色版）

主　编　付俊玲　王锦俞

副主编　詹慧贞　朱　列

参　编　邹军新　王春红　张　闽

主　审　姚元宁

机械工业出版社

CHINA MACHINE PRESS

本书是机械工业出版社职业教育汽车类专业"十三五"规划教材。本书以彩色汽车构造及各零部件图的英汉对照为主要方式来进行汽车专业英语的学习。考虑到职业院校汽车专业学生的特点，本书内容浅显而实用，主要包括汽车概述、发动机、发动机性能、车辆底盘、车身及附件、汽车电气和电子设备、手工具和车间设备七章，可作为职业院校汽车专业英语课程的教材。

为方便教学，本书配有大量教学辅助材料（包括电子课件、全书习题答案、全书英汉词汇表）。凡选用本书作为授课教材的教师，均可在机工教育服务网以教师身份注册、下载。编辑咨询电话：010-88379865。

图书在版编目（CIP）数据

汽车专业英语：彩色版 / 付俊玲，王锦俞主编 . —3 版 . —北京：机械工业出版社，2019.1（2025.6 重印）

职业教育汽车类专业"十三五"创新教材

ISBN 978-7-111-61615-3

Ⅰ . ①汽… Ⅱ . ①付… ②王… Ⅲ . ①汽车工程 – 英语 – 高等职业教育 – 教材 Ⅳ . ① U46

中国版本图书馆 CIP 数据核字（2018）第 289323 号

机械工业出版社（北京市百万庄大街 22 号 邮政编码 100037）

策划编辑：曹新宇 责任编辑：曹新宇 杨 洋

责任印制：任维东

北京中科印刷有限公司印刷

2025 年 6 月第 3 版第 8 次印刷

184mm×260mm · 10.75 印张 · 267 千字

标准书号：ISBN 978-7-111-61615-3

定价：43.00 元

电话服务　　　　　　网络服务

客服电话：010-88361066　机 工 官 网：www.cmpbook.com

　　　　　010-88379833　机 工 官 博：weibo.com/cmp1952

　　　　　010-68326294　金 书 网：www.golden-book.com

封底无防伪标均为盗版　机工教育服务网：www.cmpedu.com

第3版前言

《汽车专业英语》第1版自2009年4月出版以来，因其图文并茂、浅显易懂，适应职业院校的汽车专业英语教学，受到广大职业院校汽车专业师生的欢迎。和第2版相比，新编写的《汽车专业英语》第3版主要有以下两方面的改动：

第一，专为职业院校的汽车专业编写，旨在满足汽车行业对职业院校学生的基本专业英语要求，第3版大幅度压缩和简化了内容，以适应教学要求。

第二，改为彩色版，彩色插图将帮助学生更好地理解和记忆英语。

第3版的内容虽与第1版、第2版大不相同，但学习到的汽车专业词条和单词译义基本相同。同时，任课教师可在机械工业出版社教育服务网站上（www.cmpedu.com）下载大量的教学辅助材料，主要有给教师使用的PPT课件和全书习题答案，给师生共用的全书英汉词汇表等。

本书采用章节式编写方式，分别为：汽车概述、发动机、发动机性能、车辆底盘、车身及附件、汽车电气和电子设备、手工具和车间设备，共七章，35个子项。最佳为一学期70课时用；最短可适应一学期40课时的教学，即在教学中可酌情删去每节课中的阅读材料，这样内容可减少1/3、难度也会降低。使用本书时，因为要求学生具有基本的汽车构造知识，所以建议安排在汽车构造课程之后。

本书由付俊玲、王锦俞担任主编，詹慧贞、朱列担任副主编。编写分工如下：第1章和第7章由王锦俞和邹军新编写，第2章由上海市交通学校的朱列编写，第3章由江西科技学院（蓝天技术学院）的詹慧贞编写，第4~6章由内蒙古的付俊玲编写；王春红和张闽参与了本书的部分编写工作。全书由共青科技职业学院高级工程师姚元宁主审。

本书第3版继承和发扬了第1版、第2版的格式和内容的长处，在第3版出版之际向参与第1、第2版编写的高武、王成亮、李鹤、谢宁、范海燕、许建忠、郑婷芳和华老师表示感谢。

由于编者水平有限，书中不足之处在所难免，敬请指正。对本书的任何编写意见或建议请与王锦俞联系，QQ：596653837，手机：15800539896。

编　者

第2版前言

《汽车专业英语》第1版自2009年4月出版后，因其图文并茂、浅显易懂，适应职业院校的汽车专业英语教学，所以受到了广大职业院校汽车专业师生的欢迎，截至2013年1月，已印刷7次。随着汽车技术的发展，教材内容及插图应当适时更新，以贴合当前的行业实际；同时，在使用过程中，也发现了本书中某些内容过深、部分章节习题过少以及某些中、英文存在错误，所以编者在搜集并分析了大量反馈意见的基础上，对《汽车专业英语》进行了修订再版。第2版秉承了第1版的编写宗旨：采用看图认记汽车英语单词和词汇、对照阅读典型英语资料和做练习题来巩固提高的学习方法；注重趣味性、直观性和实用性，以提高学生的学习兴趣来提高学习效果。第2版中，改换了内容偏陈旧的插图和文字，调整了部分内容和习题的难易程度，改正了第1版中的错误；第2版中，"本课新单词"和"生词短语注释"均改为按字母顺序排列，以方便查询。相信《汽车专业英语 第2版》将能更好地适应职业院校汽车专业英语教学的需要。

《汽车专业英语 第2版》由王锦俞、詹慧贞、高武担任主编，王成亮担任副主编，李鹤、范海燕、谢宁、许建忠、华旻、郑婷芳参与了修订编写工作。全书由姚元宁主审。

由于编者水平有限，不足之处在所难免，敬请指正。对本书的任何编写意见或建议请与王锦俞联系，QQ：596653837。

编　　者

第1版前言

职业院校的汽车专业主要培养汽车使用和维修方面的实用型人才。为了适应新时期职业院校汽车专业的教学要求，我们编写了这本浅显、简明、实用性强的《汽车专业英语》。本教材采用看图学英语的教学方式，是新形势下的汽车专业英语教材。

当今的汽车销售和售后服务市场迫切需要新一代汽车使用、维修从业者懂得一定的专业英语。因此，本教材针对的是英语基础差，不喜欢传统英语教学的学生。本教材采用看图认记汽车英语单词和词汇、对照阅读资料巩固提高的方法；注重趣味性、直观性和实用性，以提高学生的学习兴趣和满足未来从业时市场对从业者的客观要求。本书编写的目的是使学生掌握或了解常用的汽车英语单词和术语。各校在教学中可部分采用或全部采用本教材内容。因为本教材对语法阐述较少，各单元内容自成体系，所以无需按单元顺序进行教学。

本教材由上海资深汽车维修工程师王锦俞主编。第一单元由北京市政管理学校郑婷芳和华旻编写；第二单元由北京市政管理学校李鹤编写；第三单元由北京市政管理学校许建忠编写；第四单元由北京市政管理学校高武编写；第五单元由江西蓝天学院詹慧贞编写；第六单元由南昌汽车机电学校范海燕编写；第七单元由主编王锦俞编写；词汇表由江西蓝天学院詹慧贞汇编。此外，高武和詹慧贞老师还协助主编对本教材进行了汇编和修订；徐珍、万外平、高雷、宋自清也参加了书中改图和部分修订工作。同时，感谢天津交通职业学院归艳荣教授对本书进行了细致、详尽的审阅。

本教材采用看图学英语的方式，是对新形势下英语教学和英语教材编写的一种探索，我们希望能受到广大职业院校汽车专业师生的欢迎，同时也希望使用本教材的老师对本教材的不足之处加以指正并参加下一版的编写工作。

编　者

目　录

CHAPTER 6 Vehicle Electric Circuit Diagram and Charging Systems
车辆电路图与充电系统

CHAPTER 7 Hand Tools and Shop Equipment 手工具与车间设备

Overview of Automobiles
汽车概述

1-1 Overview of Automotive Structure 汽车结构概述

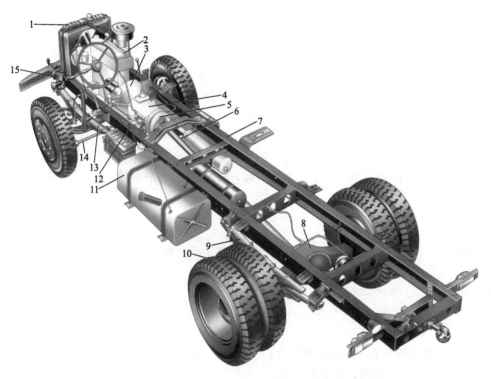

Figure 1-1   Overview of Truck Structure 货车结构概述

1	radiator	散热器,(俗称)水箱	9	rear suspension	后悬架	
2	engine	发动机	10	tire*（US）	轮胎	
3	clutch	离合器		tyre*（GB）	轮胎	
4	transmission	变速器	11	fuel tank	燃油箱	
5	parking brake	驻车制动器,手制动器	12	brake pipe	制动管	
6	drive shaft	传动轴	13	front suspension	前悬架	
7	frame	车架	14	steering linkage	转向传动机构	
8	rear-axle	后轴,(俗称)后桥		tie bar（转向系）	横拉杆	
	rear driving axle	后驱动桥	15	steering gear	转向器	

* "（US）" 表示美式英语;"（GB）" 表示英式英语。

本课新单词

automotive	[ˌɔːtə'məʊtɪv]	*adj.*	汽车的，自动的
automobile	['ɔːtəməbiːl]	*n.*	汽车
axle	['æksl]	*n.*	（轴）杆，（车辆）轴，车桥
bar	[bɑː(r)]	*n.*	棒，杆
brake	[breɪk]	*n.*	制动器，制动
clutch	[klʌtʃ]	*n.*	离合器
drive	[draɪv]	*v.*	传［驱］动，驾驶； *n.* 传［驱］动装置
engine	['endʒɪn]	*n.*	发动机
figure	['fɪgə(r)]	*n.*	图，图形
frame	[freɪm]	*n.*	构架，车架
front	[frʌnt]	*n.*	前面，正面 *adj.* 前面的
fuel	['fjuːəl]	*n.*	燃料［油］
gear	[gɪə(r)]	*n.*	齿轮，（变速器）档
item	['aɪtəm]	*n.*	项目，条目［款］
overview	['əʊvəvjuː]	*n.*	概述，概要
parking	['pɑːkɪŋ]	*n.*	驻车，停车场
radiator	['reɪdɪeɪtə(r)]	*n.*	散热器，水箱
rear	[rɪə(r)]	*n.*	后面，后方 *adj.* 后面的
shaft	[ʃɑːft]	*n.*	轴
steering	['stɪərɪŋ]	*n.*	转向
structure	['strʌktʃə(r)]	*n.*	结构，构造
suspension	[sə'spenʃn]	*n.*	悬架；悬（吊，置）
tank	[tæŋk]	*n.*	罐，槽，桶
transmission	[træns'mɪʃn]	*n.*	变速器
truck	[trʌk]	*n.*	货车
wheel	[wiːl]	*n.*	车轮

　　注：以下四个缩写表示四种常见词性：*n.*= 名词，*adj.*= 形容词，*v.*= 动词，*adv.*= 副词。其他词性，较少见，为了简明，本书未列出。

阅读材料

Cars

　　A car（or automobile）is a wheeled motor vehicle used for transportation. Most definitions of cars say they run primarily on roads, seat one to eight people, have four tires, and mainly transport people rather than goods. Cars came into global use during the 20th century, and developed economies depend on them.

　　Cars have controls for driving, parking, passenger comfort and safety, and controlling a variety of lights. Over the decades, additional features and controls have been added to vehicles, making them progressively more complex. Examples include rear reversing cameras, air conditioning, navigation systems, and in-car entertainment.

乘用车

乘用车（或汽车）是用于交通的轮式机动车辆。关于乘用车多数的定义是它们主要行驶在公路上、能坐 1~8 人，有 4 个车轮并主要用于载人而不是运货。在 20 世纪，乘用车进入全球使用并使得经济得以发展。

乘用车有用于驾驶、驻车、乘客舒适和安全的控制装置，并可对多种灯光组合进行控制。几十年来，对汽车不断增加的辅助设备和控制装置，使得乘用车日益复杂。例如包括倒车摄像头、空调、导航系统以及车内娱乐设施。

生词短语注解：

additional	[ə'dɪʃənl]	*adj.*	附加的，另外的，其他的
air	[eə]	*n.* 空气　*adj.* 空气的，风动的　*v.* 通风	
car	[kɑ:]	*n.*	乘用车，轿车；汽车
comfort	['kʌmfət]	*n.*	舒适
control	[kən'trəʊl]	*n.*	控制，操纵，控制器（controls，"控制装置"）
		v.	控制，管理
definition	[,defɪ'nɪʃn]	*n.*	定义
driving	['draɪvɪŋ]	*n.* 驾驶，驱动　*adj.* 驾驶的，驱动的	
feature	['fi:tʃə]	*n.*	特征；装置
in car		车内	
motor	['məʊtə]	*n.*	电动机，马达，发动机，汽车
navigation system		导航系统	
passenger	['pæsɪndʒə]	*n.*	旅客，乘客
reversing camera		倒车摄像头	
safety	['seɪfti]	*n.*	安全
transportation	[,trænspɔ:'teɪʃn]	*n.*	传输，运输，运送
vehicle	['vi:ɪkl]	*n.*	车辆

练习题

1. **看本课的汽车结构图，用英语读出汽车术语**
2. **单词或词组连线**

radiator	前悬架
front suspension	消声器
automobile engine	货车变速器
frame	转向器
steering gear	车架
muffler	燃油箱
fuel tank	散热器
parking brake	转向横拉杆
truck transmission	汽车发动机
steering tie bar	驻车制动器
entertainment	空调
air conditioning	娱乐设施

3. 参看下图在各序号后补上英文或中文

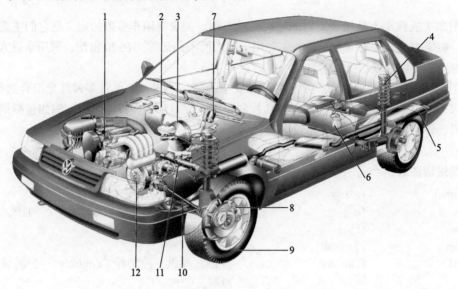

1）_____ 发动机

2）air conditioning system _____

3）vacuum-power booster _____

4）rear suspension _____

5）_____（US）消声器

silencer_____

6）_____ 燃油泵

7）wiper motor _____

8）_____ 前轮制动器

9）_____ 前轮

10）_____ 传动轴

11）power steering gear_____

12）clutch _____

4. 英译汉

1）automobile

_____

2）automobile engine

_____

3）front suspension

4）rear driving axle of truck

5）truck rear suspension

6）car rear suspension

7）steering system tie bar

8）parking brake

9）car fuel tank

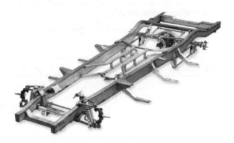

10）truck frame with suspension

1-2 Passenger Car Types 乘用车类型

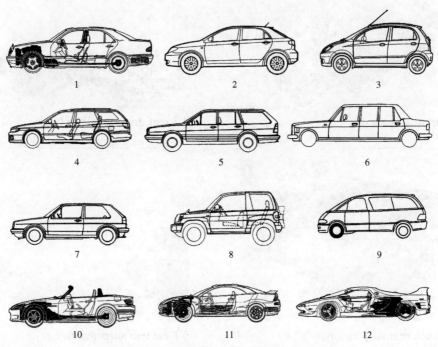

Figure 1-2　Passenger Car Types 乘用车类型

1	saloon，sedan，saloon car	乘用车，（俗称）轿车
	four door car	4门轿车
2	compact car	紧凑型乘用车
3	hatchback，hatchback car	舱背式乘用车，舱背式轿车
4	CRV=crossover（vehicle）	交叉型车
5	station wagon，WG = wagon，estate	旅行车
6	pullman saloon	高级乘用车，高级轿车
7	coupe，2-door sedan	小型乘用车，双门乘用车，双门轿车
8	RV = recreational vehicle	休闲车
	SUV = sport utility vehicle	运动型多用途车，多用途跑车
9	MPV = multipurpose passenger vehicle	多用途乘用车
	APV = all purpose vehicle	多功能车
10	convertible（saloon，car）⊖，cabriolet	活顶乘用车，敞篷车
11	sport car，sport	运动型车，跑车
12	race（racing）car	赛车

本课新单词

car	[kɑː(r)]	n.	汽车，乘用车
cabriolet	['kæbriəʊleɪ]	n.	活顶乘用车，敞篷车
compact	['kəmpækt]	adj. 紧凑的　n.	紧凑型乘用车

⊖："（　）"中的内容是词义可省略部分、说明或语境。例如："convertible（saloon，car）"表示此词条可分别写作以下三条英文词条：convertible，convertible saloon，convertible car。以下各节也同此。

convertible	[kən'vɜːtəbl]	n.	活顶乘用车，敞篷车
coupe	['kuːpeɪ]	n.	双门乘用车，小型乘用车
cross	[krɒs]	adj.	交叉的　n.　十字架
estate	[ɪ'steɪt]	n.	旅行车，客货两用车
hatchback	['hætʃbæk]	n.	舱背式乘用车
limousine	['lɪməziːn]	n.	高级乘用车（前排座与后座间可能设有隔音壁），大型乘用车
multipurpose	[ˌmʌltɪ'pɜːpəs]	adj.	多用途的
passenger	['pæsɪndʒə(r)]	n.	旅客，乘客
pullman	['pʊlmən]	n.	（火车）普尔门式车厢
race	[reɪs]	n.	竞赛，比赛
recreational	[ˌrekri'eɪʃənl]	adj.	休闲的，娱乐的
saloon	[sə'luːn]	n.	折背式车身乘用车，轿车
sedan	[sɪ'dæn]	n.	三厢乘用车，轿车
sport	[spɔːt]	n.	运动
station	['steɪʃn]	n.	岗位，场所
utility	[juː'tɪləti]	adj.	多用途的，通用的
vehicle	['viːəkl]	n.	车辆，交通工具
wagon	['wægən]	n.	旅行车，客货两用车

阅读材料

Improvements in Passenger Cars

Today's sedans are very different from the models 15 years ago. The old ones had manual door locks and windows, no air conditioning and basic audio systems. In only ten years' time, ordinary passenger cars have gained basic convenience features, advanced engine technologies and safety features.

Despite the added weight of new safety and convenience features, today's midsize cars outperform their predecessors. Engines are getting larger and have also gotten more efficient.

Performance isn't the only area where midsize cars are improving. Safety features like side curtain airbags, antilock brakes and electronic stability systems are installed in the cars. Electronic stability systems apply individual brakes when a vehicle begins to skid, in order to keep it under control. The majority of best-selling sedans have power windows and door locks, a DVD player and air conditioning. Luxury cars are typically built with higher standards than midsize cars, including the gap between panels in the interior.

乘用车的改进

现在的轿车和 15 年前的大不一样。过去的车需要人手动锁门和关窗，车里没有空调和基本的音响系统。在仅仅 10 年的时间里，普通的乘用车里有了基本的便利装置、先进的发动机技术和安全装置。

除了新的安全和便利装置外，现在的中级乘用车全面胜过了以前的中级乘用车。发动机功率变大了，效率也更高了。

中级乘用车不仅改进了性能，安全装置如侧方窗帘式安全气囊、防抱死制动系统和电子稳定系统都装配在车上。当车辆出现打滑时，为了保持对汽车的控制，电子稳定系统实施单独制动。大多数畅销车都有电动车窗、门锁、DVD播放器和空调。豪华轿车在典型结构方面的标准比中级乘用车更高，其中包括内饰板件间隙方面。

生词短语注解：

advanced	[əd'vɑːnst]	adj.	先进的
airbag	['eəbæg]	n.	安全气囊
antilock	['æntɪlɒk]	n.	（制动系）防抱死
apply	[ə'plaɪ]	v.	实施，运用
audio	['ɔːdjəʊ]	n.	声音（的）；音响
conditioning	[kən'dɪʃnɪŋ]	n.	调节；调节装置
convenience	[kən'viːnjəns]	n.	便利，方便
curtain	['kɜːt(ə)n]	n.	窗帘
efficient	[ɪ'fɪʃənt]	adj.	有效的，效率高的
electronic	[ɪˌlek'trɒnɪk]	adj.	电子的
feature	['fiːtʃə]	n.	特征［色，性］
gain	[geɪn]	v.	得（益），收获
gap	[gæp]	n.	间隙，缝隙
individual	[ˌɪndɪ'vɪdʒʊəl]	adj.	单独的
improvement	[ɪm'pruːvmənt]	n.	改进，进步
install	[ɪn'stɔːl]	v.	安装，安置
lock	[lɒk]	n.	锁 v. 锁止
luxury	['lʌkʃəri]	n.	奢侈，豪华
manual	['mænjʊəl]	adj.	手的，手动的
midsize	['mɪdsaɪz]	adj.	中等尺寸的，中级的
ordinary	['ɔːdɪnəri]	adj.	平常的，普通的
outperform	[ˌaʊtpə'fɔːm]	v.	做得比……好，胜过
performance	[pə'fɔːməns]	n.	性能
predecessor	['priːdɪsesə]	n.	（被取代的）原有事物
side	[saɪd]	n. 面，侧，一边 adj. 边的，侧面的	
skid	[skɪd]	v.	滑动，打滑
stability	[stə'bɪlɪti]	n.	稳定性
standard	['stændəd]	n. 标准 adj. 标准的	
technology	[tek'nɒlədʒi]	n.	工艺，技术
typically	['tɪpɪkəli]	adv.	代表性地，作为特色地
be different from		与……不同	
in order to		为了	
under control		被控制住	

练习题

1. **看本课的汽车图，用英语读出汽车术语**
2. **单词或词组连线**

saloon car	中级乘用车
midsize car	乘用车，轿车
compact car	双门乘用车，双门轿车
hatchback	运动型多用途车，多用途跑车
crossover	舱背式乘用车，直背式轿车
station wagon	交叉型车
executive limousine	休闲车
coupe	紧凑型乘用车
RV = recreational vehicle	高级轿车
SUV = sport utility vehicle	旅行车

3. **选填并英译汉（允许选填 2 条英文）**

hatchback passenger car, sports car, estate wagon, recreational vehicle, SUV = sport utility vehicle, 4-door saloon, convertible saloon, CRV=crossover（vehicle）, coupe, 2-door sedan, wagon, cabriolet

1)_____

2)_____

3)_____

4)_____

5)_____

6)_____

4．汉译英

1）乘用车＿＿＿＿＿＿＿＿＿＿＿＿＿＿

2）双门活顶轿车＿＿＿＿＿＿＿＿＿＿＿

3）双门轿车＿＿＿＿＿＿＿＿＿＿＿＿＿

4）旅行车＿＿＿＿＿＿＿＿＿＿＿＿＿＿

5）紧凑型乘用车＿＿＿＿＿＿＿＿＿＿＿

6）多用途乘用车＿＿＿＿＿＿＿＿＿＿＿

7）交叉型车＿＿＿＿＿＿＿＿＿＿＿＿＿

8）GT 车＿＿＿＿＿＿＿＿＿＿＿＿＿＿＿

9）高性能旅游车＿＿＿＿＿＿＿＿＿＿＿

10）舱背式乘用车＿＿＿＿＿＿＿＿＿＿

5．网上阅读题

1）从 "https://en.wikipedia.org/wiki/Honda CR-V" 上查阅对 "Honda CR-V" 的说明。

2）如果没有告诉你此网址，又该如何查阅对 "Honda CR-V" 的英语说明？

1-3 Commercial Vehicle Types 商用车类型

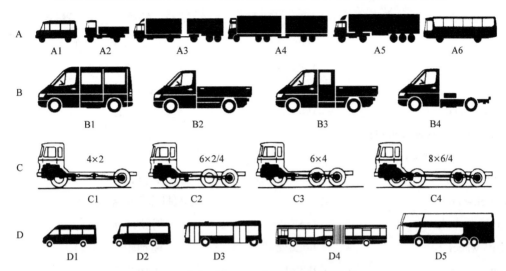

Figure 1-3 Commercial Vehicles 商用车

A	TRK=trk=truck；motor truck	（US）货车，载货汽车
	lorry	（GB）货车，载货汽车
	goods vehicle	货车，载货汽车
A1	delivery van（wagon）	厢式送货汽车
A2	high-bed flatbed truck	高台平地板货车
A3	road train，truck train（trailer）	全挂车列车，牵引杆挂车列车
A4	large capacity road train	大吨位汽车列车
A5	semitrailer train（truck）	半挂货运列车
A6	tour bus	旅游客车
B	LT=light（duty）truck，light lorry	轻型货车（目前产量最大的轻型货车是双排"皮卡"类）
B1	panel van	整体式厢式货车
B2	platform truck	平台货车
B3	double-cab low-bed truck	低地板双排座驾驶室货车
	multipurpose goods vehicle	多用途货车（在设计和结构上主要用于载运货物，但在驾驶员后有固定或折叠式座椅，可运载三个以上的乘客）
	B2，B3．PU=pickup，pick-up（truck），pickup car	客货两用车，皮卡
B4	cab and chassis	一类底盘，带驾驶室的底盘
C	system of wheels	（货车）轮式
C1	2/4 = 4 wheel × 2 drivewheel	4×2 驱动
C2	6 × 2 × 4 = 6 wheel × 2 drivewheel × 4 steered wheel	6×2 驱动 ×4 轮转向
C3	6 × 4 = 6 wheel × 4 drive wheel	6×4 驱动
C4	8 × 6 × 4 = 8 wheel × 6 drive wheel × 4 steered wheel	8×6 驱动 ×4 轮转向
D	overview of bus types	客车类型概述
D1	microbus	微型客车（按欧盟标准：19座左右、总质量为 4.5t 左右）
D2	mini bus	小型客车（按我国标准：含驾驶座不多于 17 座；按欧盟标准：25 座左右、总质量为 7.5t 左右）
D3	medium bus	中型客车（按欧盟标准：35 座左右、总质量为 12.5t 左右）
D4	articulated bus	铰接客车
	tour bus	旅游客车
D5	intercity bus，interurban bus，long-distance bus	长途客车

本课新单词

articulated	[ɑː'tɪkjuleɪtɪd]	*adj.* 铰接（的），铰链连接的
bus	[bʌs]	*n.* 公共汽车，客车
capacity	[kə'pæsəti]	*n.* 负载量，容量
city	['sɪti]	*n.* 城市，市区
commercial	[kə'mɜːʃi]	*adj.* 商用的
CV = commercial vehicle=commercial motor vehicle		商用车
delivery	[dɪ'lɪv(ə)ri]	*n.* 交货，发送
double-cab		双排座驾驶室的
drive	[draɪv]	*v.* 驾驶，驱动
drivewheel	[,draɪvhwiːl]	*n.* 驱动轮
duty	['djuːti]	*n.* 工作状态，负载，负荷
flatbed	['flætbed]	*adj.* 平台［板］式的
goods	[gʊdz]	*n.* 商品，货物，物品
large	[lɑːdʒ]	*adj.* 大容量的
intercity	[,ɪntə'sɪti]	*adj.* 城市间的
interurban	[,ɪntə'ɜːbən]	*adj.* 都市间的
long-distance	[lɒŋ 'dɪstəns]	*adj.* 长途的
low-bed	['ləʊbed]	*adj.* 低地板的
lorry	['lɒri]	*n.* （GB）卡车，货车，载货汽车
microbus	['maɪkrəbʌs]	*n.* 微型客车
midi-bus	['mɪdɪbʌs]	*n.* 中型客车
mini	['mɪni]	*adj.* 小型的，微型的
pickup	['pɪkʌp]	*n.* 皮卡，客货两用车
platform	['plætfɔːm]	*n.* 平台
PU=pickup ; pick-up		*n.* 皮卡，客货两用车
road	[rəʊd]	*n.* 路，道路
semitrailer	[,semɪ'treɪlə]	*n.* 半挂车
tour	[tʊə]	*n.* 旅游，观光
tow	[təu]	*v.* 拖曳，牵引
trailer	['treɪlə]	*n.* 挂车
train	[treɪn]	*n.* 列车
TRK=trk=truck		*n.* 货车，载货汽车
truck	[trʌk]	*n.* （US）货车，载货汽车
van	[væn]	*n.* 厢式货车

阅读材料

Definition of a Commercial Motor Vehicle

A commercial motor vehicle can be defined as:

Vehicle with a gross vehicle weight rating or gross combination weight rating of 26,001 or more pounds.

Vehicle designed to transport 16 or more passengers, including the driver.

Vehicle designed to transport 11 or more passengers, including the driver, and used to transport students under the age of twenty-one years old to and from school.

Vehicle of any size and used in the transportation of hazardous materials which is required to be placarded.

The term commercial motor vehicle will not include:

Emergency vehicles which are assigned or registered to a fire department or fire service organization when driven by fire service personnel in pursuit of fire service purposes.

Recreational vehicles.

Military vehicles when driven by non-civilian military personnel in pursuit of military purposes.

Vehicles used exclusively for agriculture and farming.

商用车的定义

商用车可定义为：

最大允许总质量或车辆总质量为 26 001 lb（1lb≈0.454kg）及以上的车辆。

设计用来运送 16 位或 16 位以上乘客（包括驾驶员）的车辆。

设计用来运送 11 位或 11 位以上乘客（包括驾驶员）和用来运送 21 岁以下的学生往返学校的车辆。

任何型号的用于运送危险原料的车辆所运送的原料名称需要告示在车辆外部。

商用车不包括：

由消防队员驾驶用于灭火任务的消防车辆。消防车辆是被指派或在消防队或消防机构注册登记的。

用于娱乐的车辆。

由军人驾驶用于军用目的的军用车辆。

专门用于农业和耕作的车辆。

生词短语注解：

assign	[ə'saɪn]	v.	分配，指派
combination	[ˌkɒmbɪ'neɪʃən]	n.	联合体，整体　adj.　组合的
civilian	[sɪ'vɪljən]	adj.	民用的，民间的
department	[dɪ'pɑːtmənt]	n.	部门
emergency	[ɪ'mɜːdʒənsi]	n.	紧急情况，突然事件
exclusively	[ɪk'skluːsɪvli]	adv.	专门
gross	[grəʊs]	adj.	总的

hazardous	['hæzədəs]	*adj.*	危险的
material	[mə'tɪərɪəl]	*n.*	材料，原料
military	['mɪlɪtəri]	*adj.*	军事的，军用的
organization	[,ɔ:gənaɪ'zeɪʃn]	*n.*	组织，机构
personnel	[,pɜ:sə'nel]	*n.*	人员，职员
placard	['plækɑ:d]	*v.*	布告
pursuit	[pə'sju:t]	*n.*	追求
register	['redʒɪstə]	*v.*	登记，注册
be assigned			被指派
be defined as			被定义为……
be required to			被需要
fire department			消防队，消防部门
in pursuit of			追求，寻求
to and from			往返于……

练习题

1. 看本课的汽车图，用英语读出汽车术语
2. 单词或词组连线

commercial vehicle	微型客车
delivery wagon	铰接客车
semitrailer	轻型货车
trailer	货运列车
mini bus	挂车
articulated bus	厢式送货汽车
light truck	半挂车
truck train	商用车

3. 英译汉

1）CV_____ 2）towing vehicle_____

3）semitrailer towing vehicle_____ 4）delivery wagon_____

5）high-bed flatbed truck_____ 6）truck-trailer_____

7）articulated bus_____ 8）LT_____

9）large capacity road train_____ 10）tour bus_____

4. 汉译英

1）旅游客车_____ 2）轻型货车_____

3）4×2 驱动_____ 4）送货汽车_____

5）挂车_____ 6）半挂车_____

7）小型客车_____ 8）厢式送货车_____

9）皮卡_____ 10）长途客车_____

5. 选填并英译汉（允许选 2 条英文）

1）mini bus   2）semitrailer   3）high-bed flatbed truck   4）semitrailer train

5）articulated bus   6）tour bus   7）city bus   8）semitrailer towing vehicle

A _____

B _____

C _____

D _____

E _____

F _____

G _____

H _____

1-4　Special-Purpose Vehicle Types 专用汽车类型

Figure 1-4　Special-Purpose Vehicles 专用汽车

	SPV=special-purpose vehicle	专用汽车
1	refuse truck，garbage truck	垃圾车
2	food truck	食品车
3	stake truck，box-stake truck	仓栅式汽车
4	tanker，tank truck	罐式车
5	van truck，box-type truck	厢式货车
6	wrecker truck，break down lorry	救援车，道路清障车
7	snow remover，snow sweeper	除雪车
8	school bus	校车，学生客车
9	ready mix（truck），concrete mixer	混凝土搅拌运输车
10	mobile home	宿营车，旅居车
11	crane truck，crane mobile	汽车起重机
12	ambulance（car，van），motor ambulance	救护车
13	container platform vehicle，container car	集装箱运输车
14	crane（lift）truck	（美）起重举升汽车
	truck with crane	随车起重运输车，随车吊
15	lifting work platform vehicle	升降台汽车
16	sweeper（truck），road（street）sweeper	扫路车
17	street cleaning sprinkler	清洗洒水车
18	fire-extinguishing vehicle	消防车
19	car repair engineering vehicle	汽车修理工程车

本课新单词

ambulance	[ˈæmbjʊl(ə)ns]	*n.*	救护车
box	[bɒks]	*n.*	箱，盒，（全封闭式货厢）车厢
cleaning	[ˈkliːnɪŋ]	*n.*	清洗，打扫
concrete	[ˈkɒnkriːt]	*n.*	混凝土
container	[kənˈteɪnə]	*n.*	容器，集装箱
cranemobile	[kreɪnˈməʊbaɪl]	*n.*	汽车起重机
engineering	[ˌendʒɪˈnɪərɪŋ]	*n.*	工程
fire	[ˈfaɪə(r)]	*n.*	火，火灾
food	[fuːd]	*n.*	食品
garbage	[ˈɡɑːbɪdʒ]	*n.*	垃圾，废物
mixer	[ˈmɪksə]	*n.*	搅拌机，混合器
platform	[ˈplætfɔːm]	*n.*	平台
ready	[ˈredi]	*adj.*	准备好的
refuse	[rɪˈfjuːz]	*n.*	废料，垃圾
removal	[rɪˈmuːv(ə)l]	*n.*	拆卸，排除；放出，移动
repair	[rɪˈpeə]	*v.*	修理
special	[ˈspeʃ(ə)l]	*adj.*	专门的，专用的
sprinkler	[ˈsprɪŋklə]	*n.*	洒水车
stake	[steɪk]	*n.*	桩，支柱
sweeper	[ˈswiːpə]	*n.*	清扫车，扫路车
tanker	[ˈtæŋkə]	*n.*	罐车
wrecker	[ˈrekə]	*n.*	救援车，道路清障车

阅读材料

What is a Special Purpose Vehicle ?

There are three kinds of SPVs: type P（plant）, type T（truck）and type O（over mass）.

Type P（plant）is a special purpose vehicle. It is primarily for off road use, for use on a road related area or on an area of road that is under construction or repair. Examples include agricultural tractors, self-propelled harvesters, bulldozers, backhoes, graders and front-end loaders.

Type T（truck）is used on roads and has no axle or axle group loaded in excess of the mass limits. These SPVs are built on a truck chassis and include cherry pickers and mounted concrete pumps.

Type O（over mass）is a special purpose vehicle on a truck chassis that is used on roads and has any axle or axle group in excess of the mass limits. Examples include mobile cranes and well-boring plant.

什么是专用车辆?

专用车辆有三种类型：P 型（重型机械型）、T 型（货车型）和 O 型（超质量型）。

P 型（重型机械型）是专用车辆，主要用于非道路作业，以及和道路有关或在道路的某个区域进行施工或修理。这类的专用车包括农业拖拉机、自走式收割机、推土机、反向铲、平地机和前端装载机。

T 型（货车型）用于道路上。这类车轴载重或轴组载荷在质量限制内。这类专用汽车建在货车底盘上，包括车载升降和安在车上的混凝土泵。

O型（超质量型）是建造在货车底盘上的专用车辆。这类车的轴载重或轴组载荷超过质量限制。如吊车和钻井车。

生词短语注解：

alteration	[ˌɔːltəˈreɪʃən]	n.	变更，改造
backhoe	[ˈbækhəʊ]	n.	锄耕机
bore	[bɔː]	v.	钻孔
boring	[ˈbɔːrɪŋ]	n.	钻孔，镗孔（bore 的衍生词）
bulldozer	[ˈbʊlˌdəʊzə]	n.	推土机
construction	[kənˈstrʌkʃn]	n.	结构，构造
excess	[ˈekses]	adj.	额外的，超过的
grander	[ɡrændə]	n.	分类机
harvester	[ˈhɑːvɪstə]	n.	收割机
limit	[ˈlɪmɪt]	n.	限制，限定
major	[ˈmeɪdʒə]	adj.	主要的
mass	[mæs]	n.	质量
over mass			超重（质量）
plant	[plɑːnt]	n.	装置，设备
pump	[pʌmp]	n.	泵，抽水机
self-propelled	[ˌselfprəˈpeld]	adj.	自动推进的，机动式的
well	[wel]	n.	井
air compressor			空气压缩机，空压机
in excess of			超过
related to			涉及，相关
well-boring			钻井

练习题

1. 读出本课的图 1~4 中英语和所有带音标的单词。

2. 单词或词组连线

special vehicle	仓栅式汽车
refuse truck	垃圾车
food truck	食品车
stake truck	罐式车
tank truck	专用汽车
box-type truck	装载高度
mobile home	厢式货车
loading height	宿营车，旅居车

3．英译汉

1）dump semitrailer train，dump car

2）wrecker truck，wrecker

3）garbage truck，refuse collector

4）container platform vehicle

5）snow removal truck

6）fire-extinguishing vehicle

7）tank semitrailer train

8）school bus

4. 汉泽英

1）车长_____ 2）总宽_____

3）装载高度_____ 4）后悬_____

5）轮距_____ 6）最小离地间隙_____

7）集装箱运输车_____ 8）救援车_____

9）救护车_____ 10）轴距_____

1-5　Careers in the Automotive Industry 汽车行业中的工作机会

Figure 1-5　Automotive service technicians can enjoy careers in many different automotive businesses.
汽车维护技师在汽车业中能享有
许多不同汽车业务工作机会

Figure 1-6　A service technician checking for a noise of a vehicle in a new-vehicle dealership service department.
新车特约维修站的一位维护技师
在检查车辆噪声

本课新单词

area	['eərɪə]	n.	区域，面积；范围
business	['bɪznəs]	n.	业务；生意
can	[kæn]	v.	能，能够，可以，可能　n.　容器
career	[kə'rɪə]	n.	事业，工作机会　adj.　职业的
checking	['tʃekɪŋ]	n.	检查；阻止物
dealership	['diːləʃɪp]	n.	代理权，经销权；经销商；特约经销商
department	[dɪ'pɑːtmənt]	n.	部，部门
different	['dɪfrənt]	adj.	不同的
garage	['gærɑːʒ]	n.	车库，修理间
independent	[ˌɪndɪ'pendənt]	adj.	独立的，单独的
industry	['ɪndəstri]	n.	工业，行业
just	[dʒʌst]	adv.	仅仅，刚刚
make	[meɪk]	n.	构造；厂牌　v.　制造，加工
many	['meni]	adj.	许多，许多的
new	[njuː]	adj.	新，新的
noise	[nɔɪz]	n.	噪声
often	['ɒfn]	adv.	时常，常常
perform	[pə'fɔːm]	v.	执行，完成
service	['sɜːvɪs]	n.& v.	服务，维护，保养
some	[sʌm]	adj.	一些，某些
specialize	['speʃəlaɪz]	v.	专攻，专门从事
technician	[tek'nɪʃn]	n.	技术人员，技师
type	[taɪp]	n.	类型
typical	['tɪpɪk(ə)l]	adj.	典型的
variety	[və'raɪəti]	n.	种种，多样性
work	[wɜːk]	n.	工作，职业　v.　工作，运作

阅读材料

New Vehicle Dealerships

Most dealerships handle one or more brands of vehicles, and the technician employed at dealerships usually has to meet minimum training standards. The training is usually provided at no cost online or at regional training centers. The dealer usually pays the service technician for the day（s）spent in training as well as provides or pays for transportation, meals, and lodging. Most dealerships offer in house on-line training.

新车经销商

大部分经销商经营一或多个品牌的汽车，他们雇用的技术人员都必须达到基本的培训标准。这类培训一般是在网上免费进行的或是由区域培训中心提供的。经销商通常要付给服务技术人员在培训期间的报酬并支付交通、食餐和住宿费用。大多数经销商提供内部在线培训。

生词短语注解：

brand	[brænd]	n.	商标，牌子
center	['sentə]	n. 中心，中央 v. 居中，集中	
cost	[kɒst]	n. 代价，费用 v. 花费，估价	
in house		室内，内部	
online	[ɒn'laɪn]	adj. 连接的，在线的 adv. 在线地	
provide	[prə'vaɪd]	v. 以……为条件，假如，提供	
see	[siː]	v. 看见，领会，理解	
standard	['stændəd]	n. 标准，规格 adj. 标准的，合格的	
training	['treɪnɪŋ]	n. 训练，培训	
usually	['juːʒʊəli]	adv. 通常，经常，平常	

练习题

1. 朗读本课的英语课文和单词
2. 单词连线

store	检查
final	经销商
user	仓库，商店
customer	容易，便利店
warehouse	部门
checking	仓库，仓储
dealership	客户，顾客
department	最终的
facility	用户，使用者
garage	车库，修理间

注：facility [fə'sɪləti] n. 容易，便利店

3. 英译汉

1）Full-service gasoline stations with an independent service shop, is a good example.

_____

_____

2）A service advisor's main job is to record the customer's concerns.

_____

_____

3）A bay in an independent service shop.

_____

_____

4）Many parts stores are part of a national corporation with stores located across the country.

_____

_____

4. 汉译英

1）汽车维护_____ 2）汽车修理_____

3）服务顾问_____ 4）维修便利店_____

5）1～2个牌号车辆_____ 6）特约维修站_____

7）车辆噪声_____ 8）独立维修店_____

CHAPTER 2 Engines 发动机

2-1 Structure Schematic of Engines 发动机结构示意图

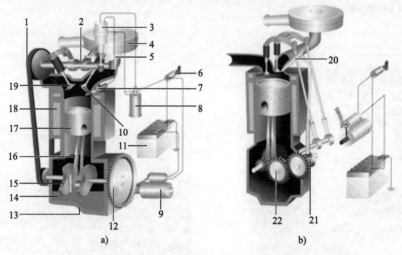

Figure 2-1   Structure Schematic of Engines 发动机结构示意图

a) Gasoline Engine 汽油机   b) Diesel Engine 柴油机

1	timing belt	正时带	12	flywheel	飞轮
2	camshaft⊖, cam shaft	凸轮轴	13	oil pan	油底壳，机油盘
3	distributor	分电器	14	oil	机油
4	air cleaner	空气滤清器	15	crankshaft⊖, crank shaft	曲轴
5	throttle body	节气门体	16	connecting rod, con⊖rod	连杆
6	ignition switch	点火开关	17	piston	活塞
7	spark plug	火花塞	18	water jacket	（冷却系）水套
8	ignition coil	点火线圈	19	exhaust valve	排气门
9	starter	起动器，起动机	20	injector	喷油器
10	intake valve	进气门	21	cam shaft	凸轮轴
11	battery	蓄电池	22	timing gear	正时齿轮

本课新单词

body	['bɒdi]	*n.*	机体；车身，（货车）货箱

⊖ 由于常用，词条变为单词，这种情况在汽车英语中较多。

⊖ 由于常用，单词被简化运用，这种情况在某些汽车英语特定词条中有。

cam	[kæm]	n.	凸轮，偏心轮
camshaft	['kæmʃɑːft]	n.	凸轮轴
connecting	[kə'nektɪŋ]	n.	连接
cleaner	['kliːnə]	n.	滤清器，清洁器
crankshaft	['kræŋkʃɑːft]	n.	曲轴
diesel	['diːzl]	n.	柴油，柴油机
distributor	[dɪ'strɪbjʊtə]	n.	分电器，分配器
exhaust	[ɪɡ'zɔːst]	n.	排气，废气 v. 排气
flywheel	['flaɪwiːl]	n.	飞轮
gasoline	['ɡæsəliːn]	n.	汽油
gear	[ɡɪə]	n.	齿轮；（变速器）档
head	[hed]	n.	头，顶，盖 adj. 头的，主要的，在顶端的
injector	[ɪn'dʒektə]	n.	喷油器
intake	['ɪnteɪk]	n.	进气，吸入；进口
jacket	['dʒækɪt]	n.	（外，水，护）套
oil	[ɔɪl]	n.	润滑油，（发动机）机油
pan	[pæn]	n.	盘，平底容器，（发动机）油底壳
piston	['pɪstən]	n.	活塞
rod	[rɒd]	n.	杆，棒，条
schematic	[skiː'mætɪk]	n.	图表；简图，示意图
spark	[spɑːk]	n.	火花；点火
starter	['stɑːtə]	n.	起动机
structure	['strʌktʃə]	n.	结构，构造
throttle	['θrɒtl]	n.	节气门，节流阀
timing	['taɪmɪŋ]	n.	正时，定时；时间调节
valve	[vælv]	n.	气门
water	['wɔːtə(r)]	n.	水

阅读材料

The Inline Engine

We all know the engine is the heart of the automobile. What is the core of the engine? Yes, it's the cylinder. Most cars have more than one cylinder（four, six and eight cylinders are common）. In a multi-cylinder engine, the cylinders usually are arranged in one of three ways: inline, V or flat.

In an inline engine, the cylinders are arranged in a line in a single bank. The inline arrangement is the simplest and most common one and has many advantages. First, the engine has a good stability and more power. Second, the structures of the cylinder block and the crankshaft are very simple and they share only one cylinder head. The cost to manufacture and install is less. Because of these advantages, BMW and also many American car manufacturers like to use the inline cylinder engine. This kind of engine is widely used in the cars made in home.

直列式发动机

我们都知道发动机是汽车的心脏。那发动机的核心又是什么？对，是气缸。大多数汽车的发动机不止一个气缸（四缸、六缸、八缸的较为常见）。在多缸发动机中，气缸的排列通常是以下面三种方式之一：直列式、V 列式和水平式。

在直列式发动机中，各气缸在一个机体中排成一直列。直列式发动机是最简单最常用的。它有很多优点：第一，直列发动机稳定性高，动力更强。第二，缸体和曲轴结构十分简单，而且使用一个气缸盖。制造和安装成本较低。正是这些优点，宝马和许多美国的汽车制造商喜欢使用直列发动机。直列发动机在国产车中应用也十分广泛。

生词短语注解：

advantage	[əd'vɑ:ntɪdʒ]	*n.*	优点，优势
arrange	[ə'reɪndʒ]	*v.*	排列，安排
arrangement	[ə'reɪndʒmənt]	*n.*	排列，安排
automobile	['ɔ:təməbi:l]	*n.*	汽车
bank	[bæŋk]	*n.*	（一）组，（一）列
core	[kɔ:]	*n.*	核（心），中心部分
flat	[flæt]	*adj.*	平坦的，平直的
heart	[hɑ:t]	*n.*	心脏
manufacture	[ˌmænjʊ'fæktʃə]	*n.*	制造
power	['paʊə]	*n.*	功率，动力；电源，能量
share	[ʃeə]	*v.*	共享，分享

练习题

1. **单词或词组英汉连线**

connecting rod	排气门
flywheel	连杆
crankshaft	油底壳
oil pan	飞轮
exhaust valve	曲轴
injector	正时带
cam shaft	水套
timing gear	凸轮轴
water jacket	喷油器
timing belt	正时齿轮

2. 英译汉和汉译英

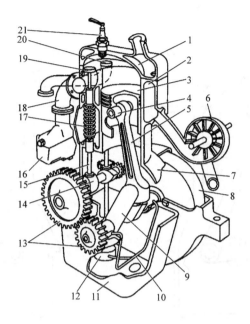

1—cylinder head_____　　2—cylinder block_____

3—_____活塞　　　　　4—piston pin_____

5—_____连杆　　　　　6—water pump_____

7—crankcase_____　　　8—_____飞轮

9—_____曲轴　　　　　10—oil pipe_____

11—oil pan_____　　　　12—oil pump_____

13—_____正时齿轮　　　14—_____凸轮轴

15—tappet_____　　　　16—_____节气门体

17—valve spring_____　　18—intake pipe_____

19—_____进气门　　　　20—_____排气门

21—_____火花塞

3. 写出 2016 年或 2017 年全球十大汽车公司中英文名称

例如：GM =General Motors Corporation（美）通用汽车公司

4. 拓展题

查出 2016 年或 2017 年全球十大汽车公司官网网址

例如：丰田官网 https://www.toyota.com/

2-2 Four-Stroke Engine Operations 四冲程发动机工作原理

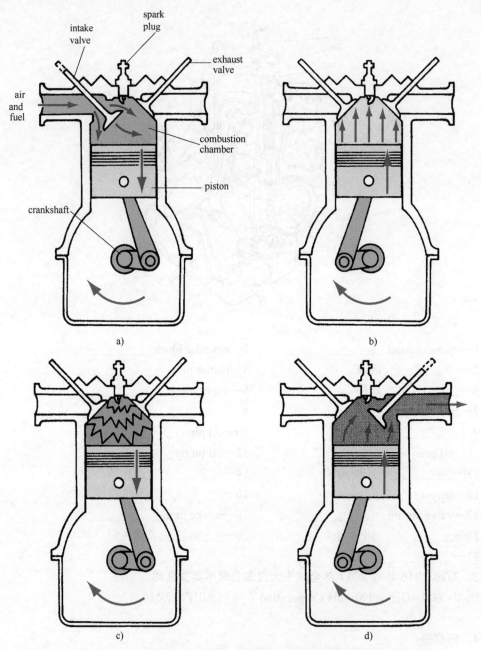

Figure 2-2　Four-Stroke Engine Operations 四冲程发动机工作原理

a）intake(suction，induction)stroke 进气行程

The intake valve is opened while the exhaust valve is closed. 进气门开启而排气门关闭。

b）compression stroke(travel) 压缩行程

Both the intake and exhaust valves are closed. 进气门和排气门均关闭。

c）Expansion(Power) stroke 膨胀（作功）行程

Both the intake and exhaust valves are closed. 进气门和排气门均关闭。

d）exhaust stroke 排气行程

The intake valve is closed while the exhaust valve is opened. 进气门关闭而排气门开启。

air and fuel	空气和燃油
combustion chamber	燃烧室
exhaust valve=EV	排气门
intake valve=IV	进气门
piston	活塞
spark plug	火花塞

本课新单词

both	[bəʊθ]	adj. 两者的，双方的
chamber	['tʃeɪmbə]	n. 室，腔，燃烧室
closed	[kləʊzd]	adj. 关闭的
expansion	[ɪk'spænʃn]	n. 膨胀
combustion	[kəm'bʌstʃən]	n. 燃烧
opened	['əʊpənd]	adj. （打）开的
induction	[ɪn'dʌkʃn]	n. （发动机）进气，吸气
operation	[ˌɒpə'reɪʃn]	n. 操作，运转，工作
stroke	[strəʊk]	n. 行程，冲程
suction	['sʌkʃən]	n. 吸入，吸气，进气
travel	['trævəl]	n. 行程 v. 移动，行进
while	[waɪl]	conj. 而，与……同时 n. （一段）时间
work	[wɜːk]	n. 工作 v. 运转
working	['wɜːkɪŋ]	n. 工作，做功

阅读材料

Main Terms

Stroke refers to piston movement. A stroke occurs when the piston moves from one extreme position to the other extreme position inside the engine cylinder. The highest position that the piston reaches inside the cylinder is called TDC（top dead center）. Similarly, the lowest position that the piston reaches inside the cylinder is called BDC（bottom dead center）. So we can also say a stroke is piston movement from TDC to BDC or vice versa. During the induction stroke, the volume of air/fuel mixture to fill a single cylinder is swept by the piston; this volume is called the swept volume. During the compression stroke, the swept volume is compressed into a small space above the piston. And at this time, the piston reaches the top of the cylinder. The space is called as the clearance volume. The clearance volume and the swept volume determine the compression ratio.

主要术语

行程是指活塞的运动。活塞在气缸里从一头运行到另一头完成一次行程。活塞运行到的最高点叫上止点。同样，活塞运行到的最低点叫下止点。因此我们也可以说一次行程就是活塞从上止点到下止点或从下止点到上止点的运行过程。在进气行程中，活塞扫过的气缸里燃油混合气的容积叫作工作容积。在压缩行程中，活塞到达上止点时，活塞顶面上方气缸工作容积被压缩后形成的容积称为燃烧室容积。燃烧室容积和气缸工作容积决定压缩比。

生词短语注解：

call	[kɔːl]	v.	称作
describe	[dɪ'skraɪb]	v.	描写，叙述
determine	[dɪ'tɜːmɪn]	v.	决定，确定
extreme	[ɪk'striːm]	adj.	尽头的，极端的
highest	[haɪɪst]	adj.	最高的（high 的最高级）
induction	[ɪn'dʌkʃn]	n.	（发动机）进气，吸气
lowest	['ləʊɪst]	adj.	最低的（low 的最高级）
main	[meɪn]	adj.	主（要）的，总的
mixture	['mɪkstʃə]	n.	混合物
move	[muːv]	v.	移动，运行
movement	['muːvmənt]	n.	运动，运行
occur	[ə'kɜː]	v.	发生，出现
performance	[pə'fɔːməns]	n.	性能，工作情况
position	[pə'zɪʃn]	n.	位置
similarly	['sɪmələli]	adv.	同样地，类似于
term	[tɜːm]	n.	术语；期间
clearance volume			余隙容积，（内燃机）燃烧室容积
from…to…			从……到……
refer to			提及，指的是
swept volume			（气缸）工作容积，气缸排量
vice versa			反之亦然

练习题

1. 英译汉

1）TDC_____

2）BDC_____

3）swept volume_____

4）compression ratio_____

5）exhaust_____

6）stroke_____

7）clearance volume_____

8）intake valve closed_____

9）EV_____

10）IV_____

2. 英汉连线

gasoline engine	工作容积
compression travel	活塞行程
exhaust valve	下止点
intake valve	排气门
swept volume	汽油机
bottom dead center	进气门
piston travel	压缩行程
clearance volume	压缩比
compression ratio	燃烧室容积

3. 汉译英

1）气缸工作容积_____

2）下止点_____

3）上止点_____

4）气门关闭_____

5）四冲程发动机_____

6）燃烧室容积_____

7）进气门开启_____

8）活塞运动_____

4. 写出中国十大汽车公司中英文名称（含合资公司）

例如：上海大众汽车有限公司 Shanghai Volkswagen Automotive Company

2-3 Structure of an Engine发动机的结构

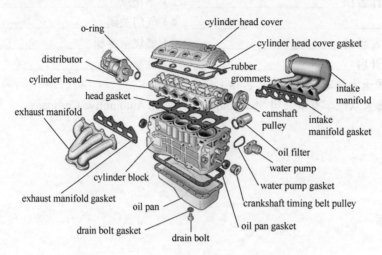

Figure 2-3 Engine Exploded View 发动机分解图

The engine provides the power to drive the wheels of the vehicle. All automobile engines, both gasoline and diesel, are classified as internal combustion engines. Combustion is the burning of an air and fuel mixture.

发动机提供驱动车轮的动力。所有汽车发动机，汽油机和柴油机这两种，都归类为内燃机。燃烧就是空气和燃油的混合气在燃烧。

camshaft pulley	凸轮轴带轮	head gasket	气缸盖衬垫
crankshaft timing belt pulley	曲轴正时带轮	intake manifold	进气歧管
cylinder block	缸体，气缸体	intake manifold gasket	进气歧管衬垫
cylinder head	气缸盖	oil filter	机油滤清器
cylinder head cover	气缸盖罩	oil pan	油底壳
cylinder head cover gasket	气缸盖罩衬垫	oil pan gasket	油底衬垫
distributor	分电器，分配器	o-ring	O形圈
drain bolt	放油螺栓（常用：drain plug 放油塞，放泄塞［龙头］）	rubber grommet	橡胶护孔圈
drain bolt gasket	放油螺栓垫片	water pump	水泵
exhaust manifold	排气歧管	water pump gasket	水泵衬垫
exhaust manifold gasket	排气歧管衬垫		

本课新单词

explode	[ɪk'spləʊd]	v.	爆炸［发］
rubber	['rʌbə(r)]	n.	橡胶
grommet	['grɒmɪt]	n.	护孔圈［环，套，管］
plug	[plʌg]	n.	塞，龙头
drain	[dreɪn]	n.	排泄 v. 排出，放泄

provide	[prə'vaɪd]	v.	提供，供应
classified	['klæsɪfaɪd]	adj.	（已）分类的
internal	[ɪn'tɜ:nl]	adj.	内部的
combustion	[kəm'bʌstʃən]	n.	燃烧
burning	['bɜ:nɪŋ]	adj.	燃烧；燃烧的

阅读材料

Cylinder Head

The cylinder head fastens to the top of the block, just as a roof of a house. The underside forms the combustion chamber with the top of the piston. The cylinder head carries the valves, and it has ports to allow air, fuel, and exhaust move through the engine. Like the cylinder block, the head is made from either cast iron or aluminum alloy.

The cylinder head is attached to the block with high-tensile steel studs. The joint between the block and the head must be gas-tight so that none of the burning mixture can escape. Thus, a gasket is used. Head gaskets are made of thin sheets of soft metal or of asbestos and metal. Gaskets are also used to seal joints between other parts, such as between the oil pan, manifolds, or water pump and the block.

气缸盖

气缸盖固定在缸体的上部，就像房子的房顶一样。缸盖的下部和活塞的顶部组成了燃烧室。缸盖上有气门，还有让空气、燃油以及废气进出的进排气口。和气缸体一样，缸盖也是由铸铁或铝合金铸造的。

气缸盖使用高强度的钢制螺栓和缸体固定在一起。缸体和缸盖之间必须密封紧密，这样燃烧的混合气才不会逸出。因此必须安装密封垫。缸盖上的密封垫是用软金属片或石棉和金属片制成的。密封垫也用在其他零件之间，如油底壳、歧管或水泵与缸体的密封上。

生词短语注解：

alloy	['ælɒɪ]	n.	合金
aluminum	[ˌæljʊ'mɪnɪəm]	n.	铝
asbestos	[æz'bestɒs]	n.	石棉
attach	[ə'tætʃ]	v.	附着，连接
cast	[kɑ:st]	v.	浇注，铸造
escape	[ɪ'skeɪp]	v.	排出，逸出
fasten	['fɑ:s(ə)n]	v.	固定，紧固
form	[fɔ:m]	v.	形成，构成
gas-tight	['gæsˌtaɪt]	adj.	不漏气的，耐气构造的
iron	['aɪən]	n.	铁

joint	[dʒɔɪnt]	*n.* 接缝，接合点
metal	['metl]	*n.* 金属
roof	[ru:f]	*n.* 顶，顶部
sheet	[ʃi:t]	*n.* 薄板，（一）片（张）
soft	[sɒft]	*adj.* 软的，柔软的
steel	[sti:l]	*n.* 钢，钢铁
tensile	['tensaɪl]	*adj.* 抗拉的，张力的
thin	[θɪn]	*adj.* 薄的，微薄的
underside	['ʌndəsaɪd]	*n.* 下面，内面
be attached to		附着在 / 连接到 / 固定在……上
be made from		由……制成
between...and...		在……和……之间（两者之间）
either...or		要么……要么……，或者……（两者中的任一个）

练习题

1. **英汉连线**

hydraulic tappet	内燃机
oil release valve	催化转化器
exhaust manifold gasket	放油塞
valve tappet	机油释压阀
used car	护孔圈
camshaft timing belt pulley	二手车
grommet	液压挺柱
catalytic converter	凸轮轴正时带轮
drain plug	气门挺柱
internal combustion engine	排气歧管衬垫

2. **汉译英**

1）机油泵＿＿＿＿＿＿＿＿＿＿＿　2）正时带＿＿＿＿＿＿＿＿＿＿＿

3）放油塞＿＿＿＿＿＿＿＿＿＿＿　4）油底壳＿＿＿＿＿＿＿＿＿＿＿

5）内燃机＿＿＿＿＿＿＿＿＿＿＿　6）橡胶＿＿＿＿＿＿＿＿＿＿＿

7）气缸盖＿＿＿＿＿＿＿＿＿＿＿　8）进气歧管衬垫＿＿＿＿＿＿＿＿

9）正时带轮＿＿＿＿＿＿＿＿＿＿　10）分配器，分电器＿＿＿＿＿＿＿

3. 英译汉

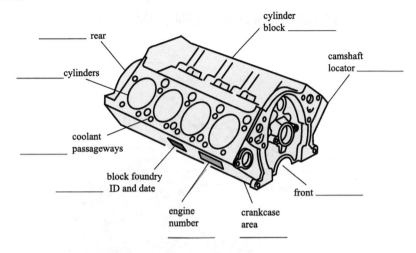

注：ID=identification 识别　area　区域，领域，范围　passageway　通路，通道
思考：图中为什么有的单词用复数？

4. 拓展题

写出德国三大汽车公司中英文名称。

2-4 Crankshaft and Connecting Rod Mechanism，Valve Train 曲轴连杆机构、配气机构

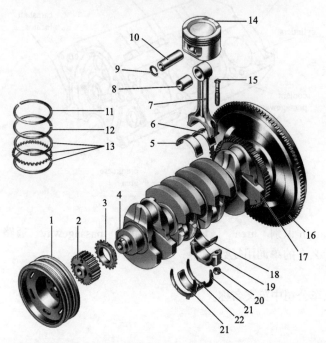

Figure 2-4　Crankshaft and Connecting Rod Mechanism 曲轴连杆机构

1	crankshaft pulley	曲轴带轮
2	crankshaft timing belt pulley	曲轴正时带轮
3	crankshaft sprocket	曲轴链轮
4	crankshaft	曲轴
5	crankshaft upper bearing	曲轴上轴承
6	connecting rod top bearing	连杆上轴承
7	connecting rod	连杆
8	connecting rod lower bearing	连杆下轴承
9	piston pin retaining ring	活塞销挡圈
10	piston pin	活塞销
11	⊖RING,CMPRN UPR = compression upper ring	第一道气环，上压缩环
	top compression ring	第一道气环，上压缩环
12	⊖RING, CMPRN LWR = compression lower ring	第二道气环，下压缩环
13	oil ring	油环
14	piston	活塞
15	connecting rod bolt	连杆螺栓
16	flywheel	飞轮

⊖ 这种大写字母缩略式词条是某些配件目录（如 GM）上的用法，后同。

（续）

17	ring of crankshaft position sensor	曲轴位置传感器圈
18	connecting rod lower bearing	连杆下轴承
19	connecting rod bearing cap	连杆轴承盖
20	connecting rod nut	连杆螺母
21	crankshaft thrust halfring	曲轴止推半环
22	crankshaft lower bearing	曲轴下轴承

本课新单词（一）

GM =General Motors Corporation			（美）通用汽车公司
bearing	['beərɪŋ]	n.	轴承，支承
bolt	[bəʊlt]	n.	螺栓
corporation	[ˌkɔːpəˈreɪʃn]	n.	股份公司，公司
general	['dʒenrəl]	adj.	综合的，通用的
halfring	[hɑːf rɪŋ]	n.	半环
lower	['ləʊə(r)]	adj.	下部的；低级的
mechanism	['mekənɪzəm]	n.	机构，机械
nut	[nʌt]	n.	螺母
retaining	[rɪˈteɪnɪŋ]	v.	保持［留，有］，维［支］持
ring	[rɪŋ]	n.	圈，环（形物）
thrust	[θrʌst]	v.	推，插入　n. 推力
upper	['ʌpə(r)]	adj.	上面的；高级的

阅读材料

Engine Design

Modern engines are designed to meet the performance and fuel efficiency demands of the public. Most are made of lightweight, noniron materials（for example, aluminum, magnesium, fiber-reinforced plastics）; and with fewer and smaller fasteners to hold things together. Fewer fasteners are made possible due to joint designs that optimize loading patterns. Each engine type has its own distinct personality, based on construction materials, casting configurations, and design.

发动机设计

现代发动机的设计要适应公众对性能和燃油效率的要求。大多数用轻质、无铁材料（如铝、镁、纤维增强塑料）制造；并用较少、较小的紧固件进行组合。紧固件的减少在于对载荷进行优化的连接设计。各类型发动机都有自己的特性，这种特性是基于材料结构、铸件结构及设计的。

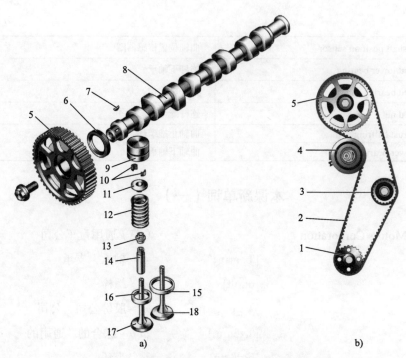

Figure 2-5 Valve Train 配气机构

a）Valve Mechanism 配气机构 b）Timing Gear 正时机构

1	crankshaft timing pulley	曲轴正时带轮
2	timing belt	正时带
	toothed timing belt	正时齿带
3	water pump toothed belt pulley	水泵齿带轮
4	tensioner pulley	张紧（带）轮
5	camshaft timing pulley	凸轮轴正时带轮
6	camshaft seal	凸轮轴油封
7	woodruff key	半圆键
8	camshaft（CM/SHF）	凸轮轴
9	tappet	挺柱
	valve lifter（LIFTER, VLV）	气门液压挺柱
10	valve key（KEY, VLV STEM）	气门锁片
11	valve spring seat	气门弹簧座
	spring retainer	气门弹簧保持器
12	valve spring	气门弹簧
13	valve stem seal（SEAL, VLV STEM OIL）	气门油封
14	valve guide（GUIDE, VLV）	气门导管
15、16	valve seat ring	气门座圈
17	exhaust valve（EXH VLV）	排气门
18	intake valve	进气门

本课新单词（二）

guide	[gaɪd]	*n.*	导管
key	[ki:]	*n.*	键,（气门）锁片
lifter	['lɪftə]	*n.*	挺柱
retainer	[rɪ'teɪnə(r)]	*n.*	保持［定位，夹持］器，保持架
seat	[si:t]	*n.*	座；座椅，座位
stem	[stem]	*n.*	杆
tappet	['tæpɪt]	*n.*	挺柱
woodruff key			半圆键

练习题

1. 英译汉

1）IV_____ 2）EV_____

3）thrust bearing_____ 4）crank shaft #1 bearing cap_____

5）gasoline engine_____ 6）exhaust-gas recirculation_____

7）timing belt_____ 8）KEY, VLV STEM_____

9）upper bearing_____ 10）engine components_____

2. 英译汉

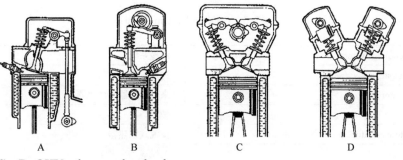

A   B   C   D

A，B，C，D OHV=ohv=overhead valves_____

B，C，D OHC=overhead camshaft_____

B，C SOHC=single overhead camshaft_____

D DOHC=dohc=double overhead cam shaft_____

3. 汉译英

1）止推半环_____ 2）活塞冲程_____

3）传感器_____ 4）燃烧室_____

5）曲柄角_____ 6）轴承盖_____

7）活塞位移_____ 8）气缸总容积_____

9）油道_____ 10）曲轴位置传感器_____

4. 写出通用汽车公司各分部中英文名称

例如：Chevrolet 雪佛兰

5. 写出美国三大汽车公司中英文名称

2-5 Cooling System and Lubrication System
冷却系统和润滑系统

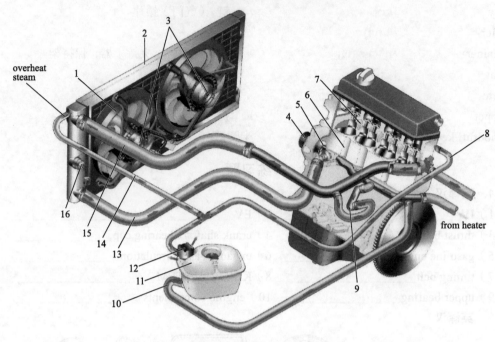

Figure 2-6 Cooling System 冷却系统

	liquid cooling system	液冷系统
	overheat steam	过热蒸汽
	from heater	来自取暖器（加热器）
1	shield	护罩
2	cross flow radiator	横流式散热器
3	electric fan	电风扇
4	belt pulley	带轮
5	water pump，coolant pump	水泵
6	cylinder block jacket	气缸体水套
7	water passage of cylinder head	气缸盖水道
8	jacket bleeding hose	水套排气软管
9	throttle hot hose	节流热管
10	reservoir tank hose	膨胀箱软管
11	expansion tank, reservoir tank ⊖	膨胀箱
12	reservoir tank cap	膨胀箱盖
13	outlet hose	出水软管
14	radiator bleeding hose	散热器排气软管
15	inlet hose	进水软管
16	thermal switch of electric fan	电风扇温控开关

⊖ 直译是"贮液箱"，但为统一，仍可译为"膨胀箱"。

本课新单词

bleed	['bli:d]	*v.*	放气，排气
cooling	['ku:lɪŋ]	*n.* 冷却 *adj.* 冷却的	
electric	[ɪ'lektrɪk]	*adj.* 电［动］的	
expansion	[ɪk'spænʃn]	*n.*	膨胀
fan	[fæn]	*n.*	风扇
flow	[fləʊ]	*n.* 流（动）；流量 *v.* 流动	
heater	['hi:tə(r)]	*n.*	加热器，取暖器
hose	[həʊz]	*n.*	软管
inlet	['ɪnlet]	*n.* 进口，入口 *v.* 进入［气，油，液］	
liquid	['lɪkwɪd]	*n.*	液体
outlet	['aʊtlet]	*n.* 出口，排出口，排气口 *v.* 排出［气，油，液］，输出	
overheat	[ˌəʊvə'hi:t]	*n.*	过热
passage	['pæsɪdʒ]	*n.*	通道，通路
radiator	['reɪdɪeɪtə(r)]	*n.*	散热器，（俗称）水箱
reservoir	['rezəvwɑ:(r)]	*n.*	储存罐［容器］
shield	[ʃi:ld]	*n.*	护板［罩］，防护物
steam	[sti:m]	*n.*	蒸汽
switch	[swɪtʃ]	*n.*	开关
thermal	['θɜ:ml]	*adj.*	热（量）的，由于热的
water	['wɔ:tə(r)]	*n.*	水

阅读材料

Engine Lubrication System

The engine has many moving parts. The purpose of the lubrication system is to supply lubricant, the oil to all the moving parts of the engine. At the same time, the system separates their surfaces, reduce friction and act as a coolant and detergent.

The lubrication system includes the following parts: the oil pan, oil pump, main oil galleries, oil filters, oil pressure relief valves, oil cooler and oil sensors. The purpose of the oil pan is to hold the excess oil during operation and non-running conditions. The oil pump is to delivering an adequate volume of oil around the engine at a suitable pressure. The oil pump operates all the time when the engine is running. Oil filter is used to filter and clean the dirt particles getting into the oil when the engine runs. A pressure regulator valve is used to keep the pressure within the oil system at a constant maximum value. The oil cooler helps to keep the oil cool. Oil pressure sensors are used to indicate the right amount of pressure of the oil system.

发动机润滑系统

发动机有许多可运动的零件。润滑系统的作用就是为这些运动零件提供润滑剂。同时，润滑剂使两个运动的零件表面分离开来，减少它们之间的摩擦并作为冷却液和清洁剂。

　　润滑系统由以下几部分组成：油底壳、机油泵、主油道、机油滤清器、机油限压阀、机油冷却器和机油传感器。油底壳的作用是在发动机运转和非运转情况下储存额外的机油。机油泵的作用是在适当的压力下给发动机运送适量的润滑油。发动机运转时机油泵也同时在工作。机油滤清器用来滤除和清洁发动机运转时带进机油的尘埃和杂质。调压阀用来保持润滑系统中最大的压力保持不变。机油冷却器使得机油冷却。油压传感器用来显示润滑系统的适量的压力。

生词短语注解：

act	[ækt]	v.	担任，充当
adequate	['ædɪkwət]	adj.	适当的，足够的
condition	[kən'dɪʃ(ə)n]	n.	情况，状态
constant	['kɒnst(ə)nt]	adj.	不变的，持续的
coolant	['kuːlənt]	n.	冷却液，散热剂
cooler	['kuːlə]	n.	冷却器
detergent	[dɪ'tɜːdʒ(ə)nt]	n.	清洁剂，去垢剂
dirt	[dɜːt]	n.	污垢，尘土
excess	[ɪk'ses]	n.	超过，超额　adj. 额外的，过量的
following	['fɒləʊɪŋ]	adj.	下列的，其次的
friction	['frɪkʃ(ə)n]	n.	摩擦，摩擦力
indicate	['ɪndɪkeɪt]	v.	指示，显示
lubricant	['luːbrɪkənt]	n.	滑润剂
moving	['mʊvɪŋ]	adj.	移［活，运，］动的
particle	['pɑːtɪk(ə)l]	n.	微粒
reduce	[rɪ'djuːs]	v.	减少，降低
regulator	['regjʊleɪtə]	n.	调节器
separate	['sepəreɪt]	adj.	分开的，分离的
suitable	['suːtəbl]	adj.	适当的，相应的
supply	[sə'plaɪ]	v.	供给，提供
value	['væljuː]	n.	值，价值
act as			充当；起……作用
all the time			一直
non-running condition			非运行状态

练习题

1. 汉译英

1）润滑系统＿＿＿＿＿＿＿＿＿＿＿＿＿　2）滤清器＿＿＿＿＿＿＿＿＿＿＿＿＿

3）散热器＿＿＿＿＿＿＿＿＿＿＿＿＿　4）机油泵＿＿＿＿＿＿＿＿＿＿＿＿＿

5）主油道＿＿＿＿＿＿＿＿＿＿＿＿＿　6）油底壳＿＿＿＿＿＿＿＿＿＿＿＿＿

7）润滑油＿＿＿＿＿＿＿＿＿＿＿＿＿　8）释压阀＿＿＿＿＿＿＿＿＿＿＿＿＿

9）冷却液＿＿＿＿＿＿＿＿＿＿＿＿＿　10）加机油口盖＿＿＿＿＿＿＿＿＿＿

2. 英译汉

1）relief valve_____   2）drain plug_____

3）oil filter_____   4）oil pressure switch_____

5）lubrication oil_____   6）bleeding hose_____

7）shield_____   8）cross flow radiator_____

9）main oil galley_____   10）thermal switch_____

3. 英译汉

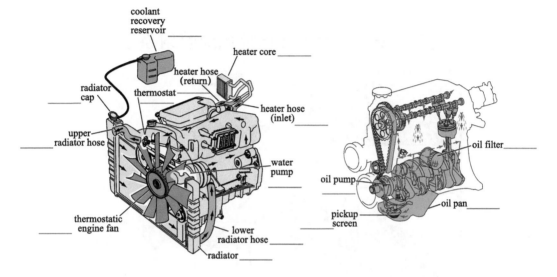

CHAPTER 3

Engine Performance
发动机性能

3-1 EFI System 电控燃油喷射系统

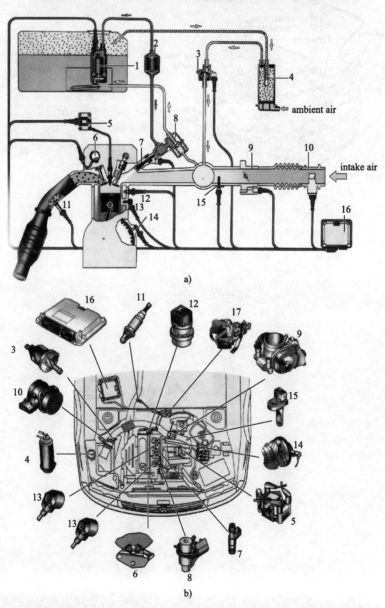

a)

b)

Figure 3-1 Electronic Fuel Injection (EFI) System 电控燃油喷射系统

a）Motronic M3.8.2 EFI System Diagram b）Components Location Diagram

a）	SFI=sequential fuel injection	顺序多点燃油喷射
	motronic M3.8.2 EFI system diagram	M3.8.2 喷射 / 点火协同管理系统图（Motronic：博世公司自创词）
	multipoint fuel injection system	多点燃油喷射系统
b）	components location diagram	零部件位置图
1	fuel pump	燃油泵
	electric fuel pump	电动燃油泵
2	fuel filter	燃油滤清器
	canister-purge valve	炭罐清除阀
3	EVAP canister purge valve	（蒸发排放物）⊖炭罐清除阀
	CANP solenoid valve=canister purge solenoid valve	炭罐清除电磁阀
4	（carbon）⊖ canister	炭罐
	EVAP canister	蒸发排放物炭罐（SAE⊖推荐用语）
	charcoal（carbon）⊖ canister	活性炭罐
5	dual spark ignition coil	双火花点火线圈
6	camshaft phase sensor	凸轮轴相位传感器（德国汽车业界用语），= CMP=camshaft position sensor 凸轮轴位置传感器（SAE 推荐用语）
	Hall sensor	霍尔传感器（大众公司用语）
7	lnjector	喷油器
8	fuel pressure regulator	燃油压力调节器
9	throttle control device	节气门控制装置
	throttle control with throttle position sensor	带节气门位置传感器的节气门控制装置
10	hot-film air-mass meter	热膜式质量空气流量计
11	lambda oxygen sensor	氧传感器（德国汽车业界用语）
	oxygen sensor	氧传感器（SAE 推荐用语）
	upstream oxygen sensor	上游氧传感器
12	coolant temperature sensor	冷却液温度传感器
13	knock sensor	爆燃传感器
14	engine-speed sensor	发动机转速传感器（德国汽车业界用语）
	CKPS=crankshaft position sensor	曲轴位置传感器
15	intake temperature sensor	进气温度传感器
16	ECU=engine control unit	发动机控制模块（德国汽车业界用语）
	ECM=engine control module	发动机控制模块（SAE 推荐用语。与 PCM 相似，但适用后驱发动机）
17	sensors	传感器

本课新单词

carbon	['kɑ:bən]	n.	炭；碳
charcoal	['tʃɑ:kəʊl]	adj.	活性的
coolant	['ku:lənt]	n.	冷却液
electric	[ɪ'lektrɪk]	adj.	电的，电动的

⊖ 实际上国内外常出现的语言简洁应用倾向；

⊖ SAE= Society of Automotive Engineers（美）汽车工程学会。此词习惯上已专指美国汽车工程学会，其他国家用 "SAE" 时都要附加国别或其他标记，如中国汽车工程学会 =SAE-China。

electronic	[ɪˌlek'trɒnɪk]	*adj.* 电子的
film	[fɪlm]	*n.* 膜，薄膜
Hall	[hɔːl]	霍尔（霍尔于1879年发现了霍尔效应，Hall effect）
high	[haɪ]	*adj.* 高（级）的 *n.* 高（度，级）
hot	[hɒt]	*adj.* 热的 *v.* 给……加温
hot-film		热膜
knock	[nɒk]	*n.* 爆燃，爆燃声 *v.* 敲，敲击
lambda	['læmdə]	*n.* 拉姆达（希腊字母中第11个字母），过量空气系数
location	[ləʊ'keɪʃn]	*n.* 位置
main	[meɪn]	*adj.* 主（要）的，总的
module	['mɒdjuːl]	*n.* 模块，组件
multipoint	['mʌltɪpɔɪnt]	*adj.* 多点；多点的
position	[pə'zɪʃn]	*n.* 位置，姿势
primary	['praɪm(ə)ri]	*adj.* 初级的，第一级的
purge	[pɜːdʒ]	*v.* 清除，净化，清污 *n.* 净化
regulator	['regjuleɪtə(r)]	*n.* 调节器
sequential	[sɪ'kwenʃl]	*adj.* 顺序的
unit	['juːnɪt]	*n.* 单位，单元，模块
upstream	[ʌp'striːm]	*adj.* 上游的

阅读材料

EFI System

The EFI system uses various sensors to detect the operating conditions of the engine and the vehicle. In accordance with the signals from these sensors, the ECU calculates the optimal fuel injection volume and operates the injectors in order to inject the proper volume of fuel. During ordinary driving, the engine ECU determines the fuel injection volume for achieving the theoretical air-fuel ratio, in order to ensure the proper power, fuel consumption, and exhaust emission levels simultaneously.

At other times, such as during warm-up, acceleration, deceleration, or high-load driving conditions, the engine ECU detect those conditions with the various sensors and then corrects the fuel injection volume in order to ensure an optimal air-fuel mixture at all times.

电控燃油喷射系统

电控燃油喷射系统通过各种传感器检测发动机和汽车的工作状况。发动机电控单元根据各传感器发出的信号计算出最佳喷油量，控制喷油器喷油，以确保合适的喷油量。在平常行驶中，发动机控制单元通过控制燃油喷射量，得到理论空燃比，以保证发动的动力性、燃油消耗和废气排放同时保持在适宜的水平。

在暖机、加速、减速、高负荷运转等其他工况下，发动机控制单元通过各种传感器确定相应工况，及时修正喷油量，以始终保证最佳的空气燃油混合气。

生词短语注解：

accordance	[əˈkɔːdəns]	n.	一致，和谐
air-fuel mixture			空气燃油混合气
all	[ɔːl]	adj.	全部的，所有的
calculate	[ˈkælkjʊleɪt]	v.	计算，考虑
consumption	[kənˈsʌmpʃən]	n.	消耗量，消耗
correct	[kəˈrekt]	v. 修正　adj.	正确的，恰当的
deceleration	[diːˌseləˈreɪʃən]	n.	减速，减速度
detect	[dɪˈtekt]	v.	探测，发现
ensure	[ɪnˈʃʊə]	v.	保证，担保
high-load			高负荷，大负荷
operating conditions			工作状况，工况
optimal	[ˈɒptɪməl]	adj.	最佳［优］的
order	[ˈɔːdə]	n. 次序，顺序　v.	定购
proper	[ˈprɒpə]	adj. 适当的，正确的　adv.	完全地
theoretical air-fuel ratio			理论空燃比
various	[ˈveərɪəs]	adj.	不同的，多样的
warm-up			热车，暖机，预热

练习题

1. 词组英汉连线

CKP	大众
CMP	歧管压力
EFI	温度传感器
ECM	节气门控制
SAE	电动燃油泵
Volkswagen	曲轴位置
temperature sensor	凸轮轴位置
throttle control	电控燃油喷射
manifold pressure	发动机控制模块
electric fuel pump	汽车工程学会

2. 英译汉

1）ignition coil_____　2）hot-film air-mass meter_____

3）electronic throttle control_____　4）intake-manifold pressure sensor_____

5）fuel pressure sensor_____　6）fuel-distribution pipe_____

7）camshaft position sensor_____　8）oxygen sensor_____

3. 英译汉

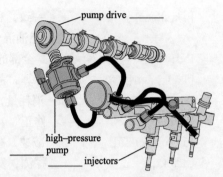

The high-pressure fuel pump for a GDI system is driven by a camshaft.

_____

NOTE：GDI= gasoline direct injection

_____

4. 汉译英

1）电子控制模块_____

2）直接喷射_____

3）多点喷射_____

4）汽车工程_____

5）汽车工程师_____

6）质量空气流量计_____

7）燃油压力_____

8）燃油泵_____

3-2　Electronic Diesel Control（EDC）System 柴油机电控系统

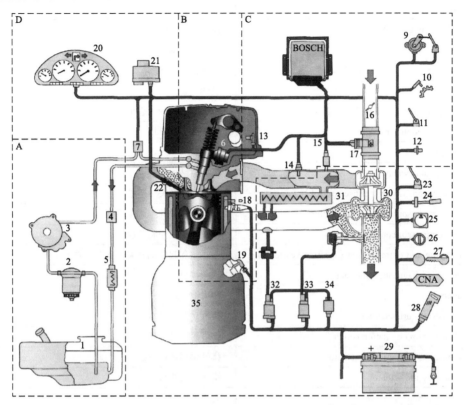

Figure 3-2　Diesel Injection System of Commercial Vehicles 商用车柴油机喷射系统

	CAN=controller area network	控制器局域网
A	fuel supply[feed] system	供油系统
1	fuel tank	燃油箱
2	fuel filter	燃油滤清器
3	fuel supply[feed] pump	燃油供给泵
4	pressure limiter sensor	压力限制器
5	fuel cooler	燃油冷却器
B	high pressure system	高压系统
6	UI = unit injector	泵喷嘴
7	fuel temperature sensor	燃油温度传感器
8	ECU=electronic control unit	电控单元
9	APPS=accelerator pedal position sensor	加速踏板位置传感器
10	VSS = vehicle speed sensor	车速传感器
11	brake light switch	制动灯开关
12	ambience-air-temperature sensor	环境温度传感器
13	CMP=camshaft position sensor	凸轮轴位置传感器
14	IATS = intake-air-temperature sensor	进气温度传感器
15	boost-pressure sensor	增压压力传感器

（续）

16	throttle	节气门
17	MAFM = mass air flow meter	质量型空气流量计
18	engine-coolant temperature sensor	发动机冷却液温度传感器
19	CKPS=crankshaft position sensor	曲轴位置传感器
D	Other	其他
20	instrument panel with fuel gauge etc.	带燃油表等的仪表板
21	glow plug control module	电热塞控制模块
22	glow plug	电热塞
23	clutch pedal switch	离合器踏板开关
24	cruise system switch（cruise control）	巡航系统开关（巡航控制）
25	A/C compressor with control module	带控制模块的空调压缩机
26	A/C compressor control module	空调压缩机控制模块
27	glow plug and starter switch（ignition-key lock）	电热塞和起动机开关（点火开关）
28	diagnosis [diagnostic] interface	诊断接口
29	battery	蓄电池
30	exhaust-gas turbocharger	废气涡轮增压器
31	exhaust gas recirculation cooler	排气再循环冷却器
32	exhaust gas recirculation actuator	排气再循环执行器
33	boost-pressure actuator	增压压力执行器
34	vacuum pump	真空泵
35	CAN = controller area network	控制器局域网

本课新单词

actuator	['æktjʊeɪtə]	n.	执行器，动作器
ambience	['æmbɪəns]	n.	周围环境
area	['eərɪə]	n.	区域，地区，面
boost	[buːst]	v.	增加，提高；（发动机）增压 *n.* 推动
controller	[kən'trəʊlə]	n.	控制者，控制器
cruise	[kruːz]	v.	巡航 *n.* 巡航
diagnosis	[ˌdaɪəg'nəʊsɪs]	n.	诊断
diagnostic	[ˌdaɪəg'nɒstɪk]	adj.	诊断；诊断的
etc	[ɪt'setərə]	adv.	等等
glow	[gləʊ]	v.	发光，灼热 *n.* （柴油机）电热塞
glow plug			电热塞
interface	['ɪntəfeɪs]	n.	接口 *v.* 接合，连接
key	[kiː]	n.	钥匙；锁片；滑块；键 *v.* 用钥匙……
limiter	['lɪmɪtə]	n.	限制器
network	['netwɜːk]	n.	网，网络
other	['ʌðə(r)]	adj.	其他
supply	[sə'plaɪ]	v.	供给，提供

阅读材料

Diesel Fuel Injection

All diesel engines draw air only, past the intake valve into the cylinder. A high-pressure fuel-injection system injects fuel into the cylinder. The amount of fuel injected is varied to suit the load on the engine, and to control engine speed. Intake air volume does not change.

In a basic diesel fuel system, a fuel tank holds the diesel fuel. A lift pump takes fuel from the tank. It keeps the injection pump full of fuel. A sedimenter removes any water, and larger particles in the fuel. A fuel filter removes minute particles. An injection pump delivers fuel under very high pressure to the injectors. It must send the correct amount of fuel, and it must send it at the correct time in the engine cycle. An injector, at each cylinder, sprays fuel into each combustion chamber. Leak-off pipes take fuel used for cooling, and for lubrication, from the injection pump and injectors back to the tank. A governor controls engine speed. And a control lever on the governor is connected to the accelerator pedal.

柴油喷射

所有的柴油发动机只吸入空气，空气通过进气门进入气缸。高压燃油喷射系统把燃油喷射到气缸。喷入的燃油量因发动机的工作状况而不同，以控制发动机的转速。吸入的空气量不变。

在一个基本的柴油机燃油系统里，燃油箱储存柴油。供油泵从油箱里吸油，保持喷油泵里燃油充足。沉淀器去掉燃油里的水分和较大的颗粒。燃油滤清器滤去细小的颗粒。喷油泵提供给喷油器高压燃油。喷油泵必须在发动机运转时适时地喷入最佳油量。每个气缸里的喷油器把燃油喷射到相应的燃烧室。起冷却和润滑作用的燃油从喷油泵和喷油器里经回油管流回油箱。调速器控制发动机的转速。调速器上的一个控制杆和加速踏板连接。

生词短语注解：

accelerator	[ək'seləreɪtə]	n.	加速器
draw	[drɔ:]	v.	汲取，吸引
leak-off	[li:k ɒf]	n.	漏气，漏水
lever	['li:və]	n. 杆，杠杆，控制杆	v. 用杠杆撬
lift pump		供油泵	
minute	[maɪ'nju:t]	adj.	微小的
past	[pɑ:st]	adv. 通过，经过	adj. 过去的
pedal	['pedl]	n. 踏板 v. 踩踏板	adj. 脚踏的
remove	[rɪ'mu:v]	v. 移动，去除	n. 移动
sedimenter	[sedɪ'məntə]	n.	（液体）沉淀器
spray	[spreɪ]	v. 喷射，喷	n. 喷雾器
suit	[sju:t]	v.	适合，相配
varied	['veərɪd]	adj.	各式各样的

<h1 style="text-align:center">练习题</h1>

1. **看本课的汽车图，用英语读出汽车术语**
2. **单词或词组英汉连线**

lift pump	泵喷嘴
glow plug	控制器局域网
pedal switch	曲轴位置传感器
ignition-key lock	巡航控制
diagnostic interface	踏板开关
pressure limiting valve	轨压传感器
rail pressure sensor	限压阀
unit injector	供油泵
crankshaft position sensor	点火开关
CAN	诊断接口
cruise control	电热塞

3. **英译汉和汉译英**

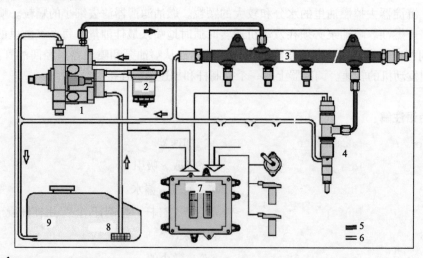

1—high pressure pump_____
2—filter with water separator and integrated hand pump_____
3—common rail_____
4—actuators_____
5—高压_____
6—低压_____
7—电子控制模块_____
8—pickup strainer_____
9—燃油箱_____

4. 汉译英

1）把燃油喷射到燃烧室＿＿＿＿＿＿＿＿＿＿　2）细小的颗粒＿＿＿＿＿＿＿＿＿＿＿＿＿＿

3）最佳车速＿＿＿＿＿＿＿＿＿＿＿＿＿＿　4）回油管＿＿＿＿＿＿＿＿＿＿＿＿＿＿＿＿

5）泵喷嘴＿＿＿＿＿＿＿＿＿＿＿＿＿＿＿　6）燃油里的水分＿＿＿＿＿＿＿＿＿＿＿＿＿

3-3 Emission Controls 排放物控制

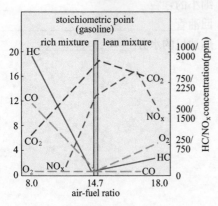

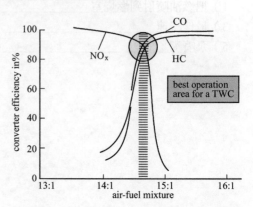

Figure 3-3   This chart shows how difficult it is to control exhaust emissions. Notice that NO_x and CO_2 are high when the HCs are low.

该图显示控制排气排放物的困难。注意，当 NO_x 和 CO_2 高时，HC 低。

Figure 3-4   The efficiency of a catalytic converter is at its highest level when there is a stoichiometric mixture.

在理论混合气时，催化转化器效率在最高水平。

converter efficiency	催化转化器效率
stoichiometric point（gasoline）	理论配比点（汽油）
stoichiometric mixture	理论配比混合气，理论混合气
air-fuel ratio	空燃比
air-fuel mixture	空气燃油混合气
rich mixture	浓混合气
lean mixture	稀混合气
concentration（%）	浓度（百分比）
HC/NOx concentration（ppm）	HC/NOx 浓度（百万分率）

本课新单词（一）

emission	[ɪ'mɪʃ(ə)n]	*n.* （发动机）排放；辐［放］射，（电磁波）发射
chart	[tʃɑːt]	*n.* 表，图表
CO=carbon monoxide		一氧化碳
CO₂= carbon dioxide		二氧化碳
concentration	[ˌkɒnsn'treɪʃn]	*n.* 浓度
difficult	['dɪfɪkəlt]	*adj.* 困难的
dioxide	[daɪ'ɒksaɪd]	*n.* 二氧化物
efficiency	[ɪ'fɪʃ(ə)nsɪ]	*n.* 效率

HC=hydrocarbon		碳氢化合物
lean	[liːn]	*adj.* 稀的 *v.* 倾斜
million	['mɪljən]	*n.* 百万
monoxide	[mɒ'nɒksaɪd]	*n.* 一氧化物
notice	['nəʊtɪs]	*v.* 注意 *n.* 注意，公告
NO$_x$=nitrogen oxide		氮氧化合物
point	[pɔɪnt]	*n.* 点，尖端 *v.* 指向，表明
ppm=parts per million		百万分率
ratio	['reɪʃɪəʊ]	*n.* 比，比率
rich	[rɪtʃ]	*adj.* 浓的
stoichiometric	[ˌstɔɪkɪə(ʊ)'metrɪk]	*adj.* 化学计算的，（发动机混合气）理论（配比）的

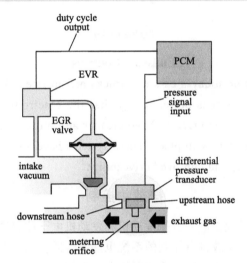

Figure 3-5   An EGR System with a Delta Pressure Feedback Sensor 带压力反馈传感器的 EGR 系统

本课新单词（二）

cycle	['saɪkl]	*n.* 周期，周；循环；回路
differential	[ˌdɪfə'renʃ(ə)l]	*adj.* 差动（的）;（有）差别［异］的 *n.* 差速器
differential pressure transducer		压差传感器
downstream	[ˌdaʊn'striːm]	*adj.* 下游［流］（的），后段［置］的 *adv.* 下游［流］（地）
downstream hose		下游软管
duty	['djuːti]	*n.* 运行，工作；负载，功用
duty cycle output		占空比输出

EGR（exhaust-gas recirculation）valve			EGR［排气再循环］阀
EVR［EGR vacuum regulator］			EGR 真空度调节器
exhaust gas			排气
feedback	['fi:dbæk]	*n.*	反馈
intake vacuum			进气真空
metering	['mi:tərɪŋ]	*n.*	测量，计量
metering orifice			计量孔
orifice	['ɒrɪfɪs]	*n.*	孔
PCM			动力系控制模块
pressure signal input			压力信号输出
regulator	['reɡjuleɪtə]	*n.*	调节器，（门玻璃）升降器
transducer	[trænz'dju:sə(r)]	*n.*	传感器（sensor）
upstream hose			上游软管

阅读材料

Emission Controls

The emission controls on today's cars and trucks are an integral part of the engine and engine control system. Perhaps it is better to say that the electronic control systems are really emission control systems. The drive to have cleaner and more fuel-efficient vehicles has led to many of the control systems now in place. These systems have also contributed to significant increases in power and reliability and improved driveability.

排放物控制

现在小汽车与货车的排放控制装置是发动机和发动机电子控制系统的一个整体部分。把电子控制系统理解为是一个对排放进行控制的系统也许更合适。能开上更环保、更经济的车辆的要求，使得更多的控制系统介入。这些系统同样在动力与可靠性方面有很大的提升，并且改善了驾驶性能。

生词短语注解：

cleaner	['kli:nə]	*n.*	滤清器，清洁器
contribute	[kən'trɪbjʊt]	*v.*	有助于
driveability	[draɪvə'bɪləti]	*n.*	驾驶性能
efficient	[ɪ'fɪʃ(ə)nt]	*adj.*	有效的，效率高的
improve	[ɪm'pru:v]	*v.*	改善，改进
increase	['ɪnkri:s]	*n.*	增加
lead	[li:d]	*n.*	引（导）线；引导
perhaps	[pə'hæps]	*adv.*	也许，大概
reliability	[rɪ,laɪə'bɪləti]	*n.*	可靠性［度］
significant	[sɪɡ'nɪfɪk(ə)nt]	*adj.*	重要的，有效的
today	[tə'deɪ]	*n.*	现在，现今 *adv.* 今天
integral	['ɪntɪɡrəl]	*adj.*	完整的，整体的

练习题

1. 单词或词组英汉连线

duty cycle	稀混合气
pressure signal	燃油压力调节器
metering orifice	浓混合气
air-fuel ratio	炭罐清除电磁阀
mixture	炭罐清除控制阀
rich mixture	占空比
lean mixture	压力信号
fuel pressure regulator	计量孔
canister purge valve	混合气
CPRV	空燃比

2. 英译汉

Evaporative-Emissions Control System

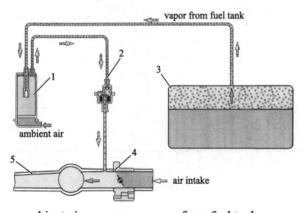

air intake_____ ; ambient air_____ ; vapor form fuel tank_____

1）carbon canister_____ 2）canister-purge valve_____

3）fuel tank_____ 4）throttle valve_____

5）intake manifold_____

3. 汉译英

1）电磁阀_____ 2）占空比_____

3）信号输出_____ 4）动力系 (power train) 控制模块_____

5）进气歧管绝对压力传感器_____ 6）再循环_____

7）稀混合气_____ 8）一氧化物_____

9）注_____ 10）氮氧化合物_____

11）点_____ 12）百万分率_____

4. 拓展题

EVAP=evaporative-emissions 来源于美国 SAE 推荐。SAE 是一个什么样的组织？

3-4 Spark Plugs 火花塞

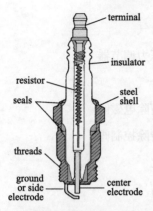

Figure 3-6　Components of a Typical Spark Plug
典型火花塞的组成

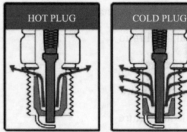

Figure 3-7　Heatrange of Spark Plugs 火花塞热值

center electrode	（US）中心电极
COLD PLUG=cold（-running）spark plug	冷型火花塞
ground or side electrode	搭铁电极或旁电极
HOT PLUG=hot（-running）spark plug	热型火花塞
insulator	绝缘子
resistor	电阻器
seal	密封剂
steel shell	钢壳
terminal	端子
thread	螺纹

本课新单词

center	['sentə]	n. （US）中心，中央
centre	['sentə(r)]	n. （GB）中心，中央
ceramic	[sɪ'ræmɪk]	adj. 陶瓷的　n. 陶瓷
electrode	[ɪ'lektrəʊd]	n. 电极
ground	[graʊnd]	n. 搭铁，接地
metal	['met(ə)l]	n. 金属
resistor	[rɪ'zɪstə(r)]	n. 电阻器
shell	[ʃel]	n. 壳
side	[saɪd]	n. 侧，旁边　adj. 侧面的，旁边的
suppression	[sə'preʃn]	n. 抑［扼］制，静噪
thread	[θred]	n. 螺纹
heatrange	[hi:treɪndʒ]	n. 热值

阅读材料

Heat Range

The amount of heat radiated by a spark plug varies by the shape and the material of the spark plug. The amount of radiated heat is called a heat range. A spark plug that radiates more heat is called a cold type, because the plug itself stays cooler. One that radiates less heat is called a hot type, because its heat is retained. Spark plugs are printed (inscribed) with an alphanumeric code, which describes their structure and characteristics. Codes differ somewhat depending on the manufacturer. Usually, the larger the number of the heat range, the cold plug, because it radiates heat well. The smaller the number, the hot plug, because it does not radiate heat easily. Spark plugs perform best when the minimum center electrode temperature is between the self-cleaning temperature of 450°C (842°F) and the pre-ignition temperature of 950°C (1,742°F).

热值

火花塞散热的大小因其形状和材质不同而变化。散热的多少称为热值。散热多的火花塞为冷型火花塞，因为火花塞本身保持较低温度。散热少的火花塞为热型火花塞，因为热量留在火花塞上，没有散发出去。火花塞上印有字母数字编码，标志其结构及特性。编码因厂家而异。通常，热值大的为冷型火花塞，因为其散热性能好。热值小的为热型火花塞，因为其散热性能差。当中心电极的工作温度在自洁温度450°C（842°F）和早燃温度950°C（1742°F）之间时，火花塞的性能最好。

生词短语注解：

alphanumeric	[ˌælfənjuːˈmerɪk]	*adj.* 文字数字的
characteristic	[ˌkærəktəˈrɪstɪk]	*n.* 特性，特征　*adj.* 特有的
cold type		冷型
heat radiated		热辐射
heat range		热值
hot type		热型
inscribe	[ɪnˈskraɪb]	*v.* 记下
preignition	[preɪˈnɪʃn]	*n.* 早燃，早期点火，提前点火（源自：pre-ignition）
radiated	[ˈreɪdɪeɪtɪd]	*adj.* 辐射的
retain	[rɪˈteɪn]	*v.* 保持，保留
shape	[ʃeɪp]	*n.* 外形，形状　*v.* 形成
structure	[ˈstrʌktʃə]	*n.* 结构
the pre-ignition temperature		早燃温度
the self-cleaning temperature		自洁温度

练习题

1. 单词或词组英汉连线

normal	正常的
hot plug	玻璃
cold plug	壳，罩，套
preignition	中心
steel shell	抑制干扰电阻
conductive	更换
suppression resistor	热型火花塞
casing	冷型火花塞
center	早燃
glass	钢壳
replacement	导电

2. 英译汉

1）a overheated spark plug

2）a wet- or oil-fouled spark plug

3）a cold or carbon-fouled spark plug

4）a worn spark plug

5）a spark plug with preignition damage

6）normal spark plug

3. 英译汉

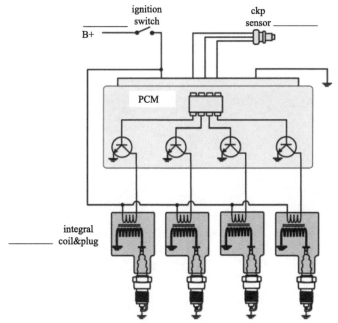

1）distributorless ignition system 无分电器点火系统

注：B+ = battery positive voltage

2）platinum（-tipped）spark plug

3）iridium（-tipped）spark plug

4．汉译英

1）中心电极＿＿＿＿＿＿＿＿＿＿＿＿＿＿　2）工作温度＿＿＿＿＿＿＿＿＿＿＿＿＿＿＿

3）自洁温度＿＿＿＿＿＿＿＿＿＿＿＿＿＿　4）早燃温度＿＿＿＿＿＿＿＿＿＿＿＿＿＿＿

5）冷型火花塞＿＿＿＿＿＿＿＿＿＿＿＿＿　6）散热性＿＿＿＿＿＿＿＿＿＿＿＿＿＿＿＿

7）热值＿＿＿＿＿＿＿＿＿＿＿＿＿＿＿＿　8）热型火花塞＿＿＿＿＿＿＿＿＿＿＿＿＿＿

3-5　Intake and Exhaust Systems 进排气系统

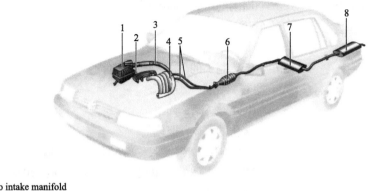

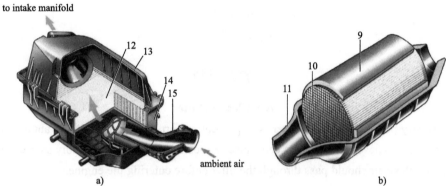

to intake manifold

ambient air

a)　　　　　　　　　　b)

Figure 3-8　Sketch of Intake and Exhaust Systems 进排气系统简图

a）Air Cleaner（Filter）空气滤清器

b）Three Way Catalytic Converter 三效 [元] 催化转化器

	to intake manifold	到进气歧管
	ambient air	周围空气
1	air cleaner[filter]	空气滤清器
2	exhaust manifold	排气歧管
3	intake hose	进气软管
4	intake manifold	进气歧管
5	dual exhaust pipe	双排气管
6	three way catalytic converter	三效 [元] 催化转化器
7	center muffler	中消声器
8	main muffler	主消声器
9	insulation	隔热层
10	ceramic monolithic	陶瓷单块载体
11	case	壳
12	element，cleaner element	滤芯
	paper element	纸质滤芯
13	air cleaner housing cover，air cleaner cap[cover]	空气滤清器盖
14	air filter bowl [box，housing]	空气滤清器壳
15	air inlet unit with sieve	带滤网的进气管组件
	intake ducting	进气管

本课新单词

ambient	['æmbɪənt]	*adj.* 周围的	*n.* 周围环境
ducting	['dʌktɪŋ]	*n.* 管道，导管	
bowl	[bəʊl]	*n.* 碗形物，杯，盘	
paper	['peɪpə]	*adj.* 纸（制）的	*n.* 纸，文件
element	['elɪm(ə)nt]	*n.* 滤芯，元件	
sieve	[sɪv]	*n.* 滤网	*v.* 滤，筛
catalytic	[ˌkætə'lɪtɪk]	*adj.* 催化的	*n.* 催化剂
converter	[kən'vɜːtə(r)]	*n.* （排气催化）转化器，变换器，（变速器）变矩器	
monolithic	[mɒnə'lɪθɪk]	*adj.* 整［单］体的，单块［片］（的）	*n.* 单块集成电路
sketch	[sketʃ]	*n.* 草图，略图	
way	[weɪ]	*n.* 路线，通路	

阅读材料

Air Cleaner/Filter

The primary purpose of the air filter is to prevent airborne contaminants and abrasives from entering the cylinders. These contaminants can cause serious damage and appreciably shorten engine life. Therefore, all intake air should pass through the filter before entering the engine.

The air filter is inside a sealed air cleaner assembly. This assembly is also used to direct the airflow and reduce the noise caused by the movement of intake air. The air cleaner also provides filtered air to the PCV system and provides engine compartment fire protection in the event of backfire.

空气滤清器

空气滤清器的主要作用是滤去空气中的杂质与砂粒，以阻止其进入气缸。这些杂质与砂粒如果进入气缸会给发动机带来严重损伤并严重地缩短发动机的使用寿命。所以任何气缸的进气必须首先通过滤清器。

空气滤清器是安装在一个封闭的空气滤清器总成里的。空气滤清器总成同时能对空气起导流作用并减轻进气的噪声。空气滤清器还能向 PCV 系统供给已过滤的空气并且 PCV 系统在发动机发生回火的情况下能对发动机舱起到保护作用。

生词短语注解：

abrasive	[ə'breɪsɪv]	*n.* 磨料，砂粒	*adj.* 有磨蚀作用的
backfire	[ˌbæk'faɪə(r)]	*v.* （发动机）回火，（排气管）放炮	
compartment	[kəm'pɑːtmənt]	*n.* 舱，室，车厢	
contaminant	[kən'tæmɪnənt]	*n.* 杂质，污染物	
damage	['dæmɪdʒ]	*v.* 损害，损坏	*n.* 损坏
direct	[də'rekt]	*adj.* 直接的 *adv.* 直接地	*v.* 指导
enter	['entə]	*v.* 进［插，加，输］入	
pass	[pɑːs]	*v.* 经过，通过	*n.* 通道
prevent	[prɪ'vent]	*v.* 阻止，防止	

protection	[prə'tekʃn]	*n.*	保护
provide	[prə'vaɪd]	*v.*	供应，供给
PCV=positive crankcase vent			曲轴箱强制通风

练习题

1. **单词或词组英汉连线**

late-model truck	滤清器盖
upstream HO_2S	陶瓷单块载体
fuel control	曲轴箱强制通风
catalytic converter	线束插座
filter bowl	电气插接器
electrical connector	当代货车
cable socket	上游氧传感器
PCV	燃油控制
ceramic monolithic	催化转化器
filter cap	滤清器壳

2. **英译汉**

1）engine backfire＿＿＿＿＿＿＿＿＿＿　　2）on-board diagnostics system＿＿＿＿＿＿

3）positive crankcase vent＿＿＿＿＿＿＿　　4）three way catalytic converter＿＿＿＿＿

5）air-fuel ratio＿＿＿＿＿＿＿＿＿＿＿＿　　6）kilovolt (kV)＿＿＿＿＿＿＿＿＿＿＿＿

7）engine compartment＿＿＿＿＿＿＿＿＿　　8）electrical connector＿＿＿＿＿＿＿＿＿

3. **英译汉**

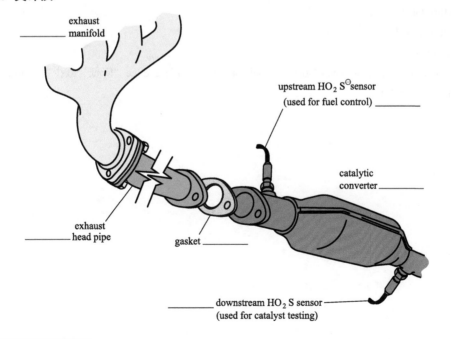

exhaust manifold ＿＿＿＿＿

upstream HO_2S sensor (used for fuel control) ＿＿＿＿＿

catalytic converter ＿＿＿＿＿

exhaust head pipe ＿＿＿＿＿

gasket ＿＿＿＿＿

downstream HO_2S sensor (used for catalyst testing) ＿＿＿＿＿

○ HO_2S sensor= HO_2S。由于目前所用的氧传感器都是加热型的，所以"HO_2S"也常译为"氧传感器"。

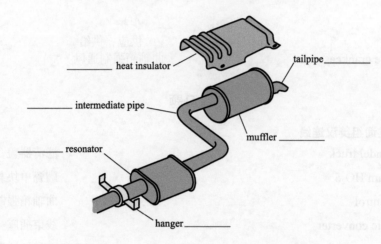

A Typical Exhaust System on a Late-Model Car

4. 汉译英

1）氧传感器_____ 2）线束插座_____

3）排气歧管_____ 4）典型的进气系统_____

5）机油滤清器壳_____ 6）冷却液温度_____

7）热空气_____ 8）周围温度_____

9）二手车_____ 10）隔热_____

5. 拓展题（英译汉）

Technician A says that the exhaust manifold gasket seals the joint between the exhaust manifold and the exhaust pipe. Technician B says that a resonator helps to reduce exhaust noise. Who is correct?

A. Technician A.

B. Technician B.

C. Both A and B.

D. Neither A nor B.

注：say（says）"说"；between "在……中间，在……之间"；reduce "降低，减少"；neither "两者都不"；who "谁"。

Chassis of Vehicles
车辆底盘

4-1 Clutches 离合器

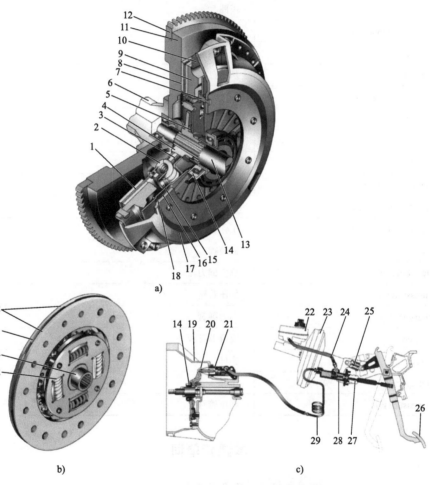

Figure 4-1   Automotive Clutch 汽车离合器

a) Major Parts of Clutch   离合器主要零件

b) Clutch Disc   离合器从动盘   c) Clutch Linkage   离合器操纵机构

1	wavy spring	波形弹簧
2	torsional damper spring	扭转减振弹簧
3	friction ring	摩擦圈

（续）

4	spline hub	花键毂
5	diaphragm spring	膜片弹簧
6	crankshaft	曲轴
7	stop rivet	限位铆钉
8	friction lining	摩擦片
9	pressure[driving] plate	压（主动）盘
10	drive strap	（压盘）传动带
11	flywheel	飞轮
12	ring gear	齿圈
13	transmission input shaft	变速器输入轴
14	release bearing	分离轴承
15	driven plate	从动盘
16	diaphragm spring	膜片弹簧
17	clutch cover	离合器盖
	clutch cover assy. ，pressure plate assy.	离合器盖总成（注：两词条为同一部件，都是带压板的盖总成）
18	pivot[fulcrum] ring	支撑环
19	transmission casing	变速器壳
20	release[operating] fork	分离叉
21	slave[release] cylinder	工作缸
22	reservoir	储液罐
23	vacuum booster	真空助力器
24	low pressure line	低压管路
25	auxiliary spring	助力弹簧
26	clutch pedal	离合器踏板
27	push rod	推杆
28	master cylinder	主缸
29	high pressure line	高压管路

本课新单词

assy. =assembly	[ə'sembli]	n.	总成
auxiliary	[ɔːg'zɪljəri]	adj.	辅助的；附属的
booster	['buːstə(r)]	n.	助［加］力器
diaphragm	['daɪəfræm]	n.	膜片
driven	['drɪvn]	adj.	从［被］动的
fork	[fɔːk]	n.	叉，叉形物

friction	['frɪkʃn]	n.	摩擦
fulcrum	['fʊlkrəm]	n.	支点，支枢
lining	['laɪnɪŋ]	n.	衬里，内衬，（制动器 / 离合器）衬片
operating	['ɒpəreɪtɪŋ]	adj.	操作的
pivot	['pɪvət]	n.	枢轴，支点［枢］ adj. 枢轴的，装在枢轴上转动的
push	[pʊʃ]	v.	推，挤 n. 推
release	[rɪ'liːs]	v.	释放，放松 n. 释放
slave	[sleɪv]	adj.	从［随］动的，从属的
strap	[stræp]	n.	带
torsional	['tɔːʃənəl]	adj.	扭转，扭转的
wavy	['weɪvi]	adj.	波状的

阅读材料

Clutch

In this article, we will learn why you need a clutch, and understand how the clutch in your car works.

The reason why you need a clutch in the car is that the engine spins all the time, but the car wheels don't. In order for a car to stop without killing the engine, the wheels need to be disconnected from the engine somehow. The clutch allows us to smoothly engage a spinning engine to a non-spinning transmission by controlling the slippage between them.

A clutch works because of friction between a clutch plate and a flywheel. The clutch is a device that lets you connect and disconnect the engine and the transmission. When you push in the clutch pedal, the engine and the transmission are disconnected so the engine can run even if the car is standing still. When you release the clutch pedal, the engine and the input shaft are directly connected to one another. The input shaft and gear turn at the same rpm as the engine.

A clutch is composed of the clutch disc, the pressure plate, the release lever and the release bearing.

离合器

在这篇文章中，我们将学习为什么需要离合器，以及在汽车上离合器是如何工作的。

汽车上装备的离合器可以使发动机与传动系统的其他部件平稳地接合。汽车工作时，发动机始终旋转，但车轮却不是这样。为了让汽车停下来时发动机不熄火，车轮必须以某种方式与发动机断开连接。通过离合器，我们可以控制发动机和传动系统的衔接行程，使旋转的发动机和静止的传动系统之间实现平稳接合。

离合器是靠离合器片与飞轮间的摩擦力工作的。通过离合器，可以实现发动机和传动系统的接合和分离。踩下离合器踏板，发动机和传动系统分离，即使汽车停下来，发动机也可正常运转。松开离合器踏板，发动机和输入轴立刻接合，输入轴及齿轮便以与发动机相同的转速运转。

离合器是由离合器盘、压盘、分离杠杆和分离轴承组成的。

生词短语注解：

allow	[ə'laʊ]	v.	允许，承认
article	['ɑ:tɪk(ə)l]	n.	文章
be composed of			由……组成
directly	[dɪ'rektli]	adv.	直接地，立即
disconnect	[dɪskə'nekt]	v.	分离，不连贯
engage	[ɪn'geɪdʒ]	v.	使从事于，参加
input	['ɪnpʊt]	v.	输入
push in			把……推入
reason	['ri:zən]	n.	理由，原因
rpm = revolutions per minute			转数／分；（发动机）转速
slippage	['slɪpɪdʒ]	n.	滑移，滑程
somehow	['sʌmhaʊ]	adv.	以某种方式；不明原因
spin	[spɪn]	v.	旋转
understand	[ˌʌndə'stænd]	v.	了解，理解

练习题

1. 词组和单词英汉连线

adjusting nut	定位器
cable anchor nut	回位弹簧
ball end	前轮驱动
clutch housing	横置发动机
linkage	纵置发动机
clutch pedal	飞轮壳
retainer	（离合器踏板）操纵机构
return spring	离合器踏板
front wheel drive	球头
transverse engine	拉索固定螺母
longitudinal engine	调节螺母

2. 英译汉

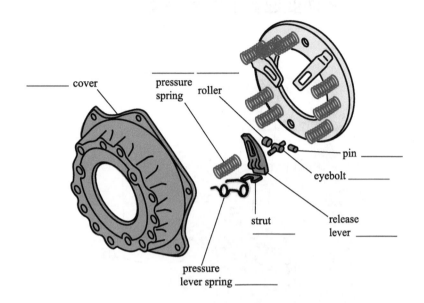

3. 句子英译汉

1）The removal and replacement of a clutch assembly can be completed while the engine is in or out of the car.

_____

2）The clutch assembly is mounted to the flywheel that is mounted to the rear of the crankshaft.

_____

4. 汉译英

1）回位弹簧_____ 2）离合器踏板操纵机构_____

3）膜片弹簧离合器_____ 4）后驱车_____

5）传动系统_____ 6）螺旋弹簧离合器_____

7）扭转减振器_____ 8）前驱车_____

5. 拓展题 / 英译汉

1）Let's check the free of the clutch pedal.

_____

2）Let's disassemble the clutch.

_____

3）There must be faults with your clutch plate, change a new plate.

_____

4）In order for a car to stop without killing the engine, the wheels need to be disconnected from the engine somehow.

_____

4-2 Manual Transaxle and Manual Transmission
手动变速驱动桥和手动变速器

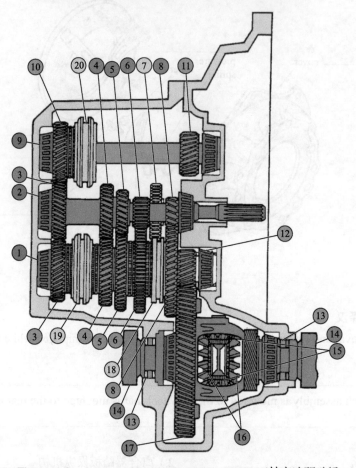

Figure 4-2   A Transaxle with Three Gear Shafts 三轴变速驱动桥

1	mainshaft	主轴
2	input cluster gear shaft	带齿轮组的输入轴
3	4th speed gears	四档齿轮副
4	3rd speed gears	三档齿轮副
5	2nd speed gears	二档齿轮副
6	reverse gears	倒档齿轮副
7	reverse idler gears	倒档惰轮副
8	1st speed gears	一档齿轮副
9	5th speed gear drive shaft	五档齿轮传动轴
10	5th speed gear	五档齿轮
11	5th gear driveshaft pinion gear	五档齿轮传动轴小齿轮
12	mainshaft pinion gear	主轴小齿轮
13	differential oil seals	差速器油封
14	CV shafts	等速万向节传动轴
15	differential pinion gears	差速器行星齿轮
16	differential side gears	差速器半轴齿轮

（续）

17	final drive ring gear	主减速器齿圈
18	1st/2nd synchronizer	一到二档同步器
19	3rd/4th synchronizer	三到四档同步器
20	5th synchronizer	五档同步器

本课新单词

1st= first	[fɜːst]	n.	第一，（变速器）第一档，一档
2nd= second	['sekənd]	n.	第二，（变速器）第二档，二档
3rd= third	[θɜːd]	n.	第三，（变速器）第三档，三档
4th=4TH = fourth	[fɔːθ]	n.	第四，（变速器）第四档，四档
5th=5TH = fifth	[fɪfθ]	n.	第五，（变速器）第五档，五档
always	['ɔːlweɪz]	adv.	总是，经常
cluster	['klʌstə(r)]	n.	组，群，束，齿轮组；仪表板
CV = constant velocity			（万向节）等（角）速；定速
final drive			主减速器，最终传动
final	['faɪnl]	adj.	最终［后］的
idler	['aɪdlə(r)]	n.	惰轮，空转［中间］齿轮，（传动带）张紧轮
mainshaft	[meɪnz'hɑːft]	n.	主轴
manual	['mænjʊəl]	adj.	手动的，手工的
mesh	[meʃ]	v.	啮合
reverse	[rɪ'vɜːs]	v.	倒退［车］，挂倒档反转　n. （变速器）倒档
synchronizer	['sɪŋkrənaɪzə]	n.	同步器

阅读材料

Gearbox

A gearbox changes the speed and torque of the output shaft by meshing different gears. It provides a way to disconnect the engine from the transmission system without depressing the clutch pedal for a long time. It enables the vehicle to be reversed.

A gearbox has many shafts and gears. The common problems with gearbox include the difficulty in engaging gears, jumping out of gear, noisy gear mesh and oil leaks. You should look for the reasons and eliminate the problems.

The diagram（see Figure 4-3）shows a very simple two-speed transmission in neutral. Let's look at each of the parts in this diagram to understand how they fit together:

The input shaft comes from the engine through the clutch. The input shaft and the gear on it are connected as a single unit.

Intermediate shaft is also connected as a single piece, so all of the gears on the intermediate shaft and the intermediate shaft itself spin as one unit. The input shaft and the intermediate shaft are directly connected through their meshed gears so that if the input shaft is spinning, so is the intermediate shaft. In this way, the intermediate shaft receives its power directly from the engine whenever the clutch is engaged.

The gears 1 ride on bearings，so they spin on the output shaft. If the engine is off but the car is coasting, the output shaft can turn inside the gears 1 while the gears 1 and the inter-mediate shaft are motionless.

变速器

变速器可通过不同齿轮的啮合改变输出轴的转速和转矩。通过变速器，无须踩下离合器踏板，就可使发动机和传动系统长时间分离。变速器还使倒车成为可能。

变速器内装有许多轴和齿轮。变速器的常见故障包括换档困难、跳档、齿轮啮合噪声大和漏油。应当仔细查找故障原因并将其排除。

图 4-3 所示是一个很简单的两速变速器，位于空档位置。让我们查看图 4-3 中的各个部件，了解其工作过程。

输入轴通过离合器与发动机连接。输入轴和其上面的齿轮是结为一体的。

中间轴也是一体的，所以中间轴上的齿轮与中间轴成一体旋转。输入轴和中间轴通过其上齿轮的相互啮合直接相连。输入轴旋转，中间轴也跟着旋转。这样，只要离合器处于接合状态，中间轴就能直接从发动机获取能量。

齿轮 1 浮装在轴承上，它们在输出轴上旋转。如果发动机熄火而汽车仍在滑行，输出轴可在齿轮 1 内转动，而齿轮 1 和中间轴则可保持静止。

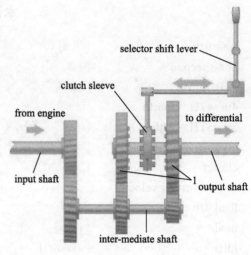

Figure 4-3　Two-Speed Transmission 两速变速器

生词短语注解：

coasting	['kəʊstɪŋ]	n.	滑行，滑下
depress	[dɪ'pres]	v.	压下
eliminate	[ɪ'lɪmɪneɪt]	v.	排除，消除
enable	[ɪ'neɪbl]	v.	使能够
jump	[dʒʌmp]	v.	跳跃，跳动
intermediate	[ˌɪntə'miːdiət]	adj.	中间［级，等］的
leak	[liːk]	v.	漏，泄漏　n. 泄漏
mesh	[meʃ]	v.	啮合
motionless	['məʊʃnləs]	adj.	不动的，静止的
neutral	['njuːtrəl]	adj.	中间的，（变速器）空档的
noisy	['nɔɪzɪ]	adj.	有噪声的，嘈杂的
part	[pɑːt]	n.	部分，零件
piece	[piːs]	n.	块，件
receive	[rɪ'siːv]	v.	收到，接收
ride	[raɪd]	v.	乘坐，骑

torque	[tɔːk]	*n.*	扭矩，转矩
whenever	[wen'evə]	*adv.*	无论何时，随时

练习题

1. 单词或词组英汉连线

speedometer	齿轮组
output shaft	倒档
transmission case	一档
flanged shaft	滚子轴承
synchronizer	五档
roller bearing	车速里程表
reverse	输出轴
5th speed	变速器壳体
1st speed	凸缘轴
cluster gear	同步器

2. 句子英译汉

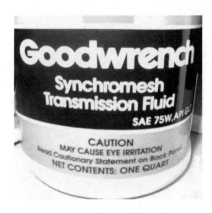

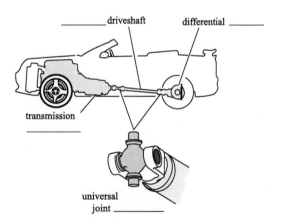

1）Some manual transmissions/transaxles require synchromesh transmission fluid.

注：synchromesh 意为 "同步啮合"。

2）A transmission mounted to the rear of the engine can be connected to the drive axle by a driveshaft with universal joints.

注：mounted 意为 "安装在……的"。

3. 英译汉

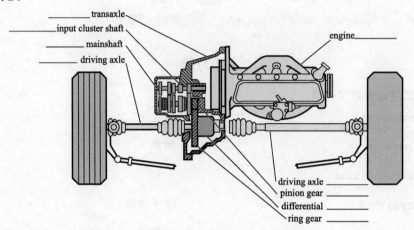

The location of typical front-wheel-drive powertrain components.

---

4. 汉译英

1）变速驱动桥_____ 2）齿轮组_____

3）手动变速器_____ 4）锥齿轮_____

5）一档_____ 6）倒档_____

7）输入轴_____ 8）半轴齿轮_____

4-3 Automatic Transmission⊖ 自动变速器

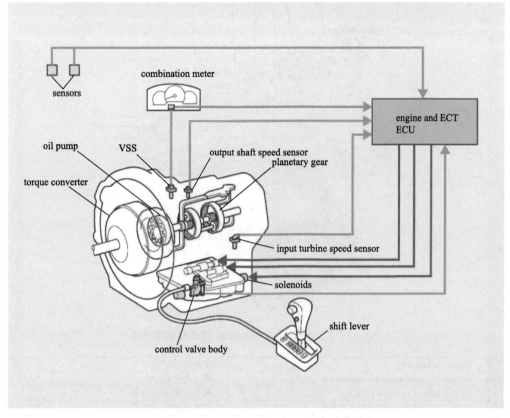

Figure 4-4　Automatic Transmission 自动变速器

output shaft speed sensor	输出轴转速传感器
combination meter	组合仪表（上有"shift range indicator light 档位指示灯"）
control valve body	控制阀体
ECT=electronic controlled transmission(transaxle)	电子控制变速器（变速驱动桥）[此为丰田公司用语，=A/T= Automatic transmission（transaxle）自动变速器（驱动桥）]
engine and ECT ECU	发动机和自动变速器电控单元
input turbine speed sensor	输入涡轮转速传感器
oil pump	油泵
planetary gear	行星齿轮机构
sensors	传感器
shift lever	变速杆装置
solenoids	电磁阀
torque converter	液力变矩器
VSS=vehicle speed sensor	车速传感器

⊖ "automatic transmission（A/T）自动变速器"实际使用中有以下两种含意：一是专指后桥驱动或全轮驱动用的自动变速器；二是包括前桥驱动用的自动变速驱动桥(Automatic transaxle) 及后桥驱动或全轮驱动用的自动变速器。

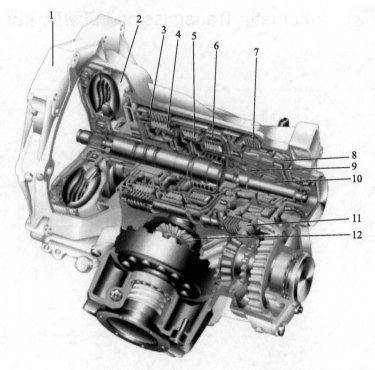

Figure 4-5 Automatic Transaxle 自动变速驱动桥

1	transaxle housing	变速驱动桥壳
2	torque（hydrodynamic）converter	液力变矩器
	TCC = torque converter clutch	液力变矩器离合器
	torque converter with lockup clutch	锁止式液力变矩器
3	brake B2	B2 制动器
4	clutch K2	K2 离合器
5	clutch K1	K2 离合器
6	clutch K3	K3 离合器
	K1, K2, K3 multi-plate brake	多片式制动器
7	brake B1	B1 制动器
8	ring gear	齿圈
9	large sun gear	大太阳轮
10	small sun gear	小太阳轮
11	planetary carrier	行星齿轮架
9 ~ 11	Ravigneaux（gear train），Ravigneaux planetary gear set	拉维列奥克斯行星齿轮机构，（俗称）拉维娜式行星齿轮机构
12	differential	差速器

本课新单词

multi-plate	['mʌlti-pleɪt]	adj.	多片的
torque	[tɔːk]	n.	扭矩，转矩
sun	[sʌn]	n.	太阳
lockup	['lɒkʌp]	n.	锁止
hydrodynamic	['haɪdrəʊdaɪ'næmɪk]	adj.	液压的，流体动力（学）的
planetary	['plænɪt(ə)ri]	adj.	行星（式）的
small	[smɔːl]	adj.	小的
Ravigneaux			拉维娜式行星齿轮机构

| set | [set] | *n.* | 一套，一组 |
| meter | ['mi:tə] | *n.* | 仪表，计量器；米，公尺 |

阅读材料

Shifting the Automatic Transaxle

There are several different positions for your shift lever:

Park :	P	Reverse :	R
Neutral :	N	Drive :	D
Second :	2	First :	1

P（Park）: This locks your front wheels. It's the best position to use when you start your engine because your vehicle can't move easily.

R（Reverse）: Use this gear to back up.

N（Neutral）: In this position, your engine doesn't connect with the wheels. To restart when you're already moving, use N only. Also, use N when your vehicle is being towed.

D（Drive）: This position is for normal driving, at all speeds, in most street and highway situation.

2（Second Gear）:（Transmission will only shift frow Low to 2nd gear）This position gives you more power but lower fuel economy. You can use 2 on hills. It can help control your speed as you go down steep mountain roads.

1（First）: This position gives you even more power（but lower fuel economy）than 2. You can use it on very steep hills, or in deep snow or mud.

自动变速驱动桥的换档

变速杆有几个不同的位置：

驻车档: P	倒档: R
空档: N	前进档: D
二档: 2	一档: 1

P（驻车档）：该档位锁住汽车的前轮。这是起动发动机时所用的最好的位置，因为汽车不容易移动。

R:（倒档）：用这个档位倒车。

N:（空档）：在这个档位，发动机没有和车轮连接。要在起步后重新起动，只能用这个档位。同样，你的汽车被拖曳时也用 N 档。

D:（前进档）：该档位适用于所有车速、大多数街道和公路上的正常行驶。

二档：2（自动变速器仅限于在 1~2 档之间进行换档）该档位带给你较大的动力（但降低了燃油经济性）。你可以用二档上坡，它能使你在下陡的山路时，帮你控制车速。

一档：1 该档位带给你比二档位更强大的动力。你可以用它来上非常陡的坡，或在深雪和泥泞中行驶。

生词短语注解：

back up			后退，（车辆）倒车
deep	[di:p]	*adj.*	深的，纵深的
economy	[ɪ'kɒnəmi]	*n.*	节约，经济（性）

hill	[hɪl]	n.	斜坡，小山
mountain	['maʊntən]	n.	山，山脉
mud	[mʌd]	n.	泥，泥泞
move	[muːv]	v.	移动
several	['sevrəl]	adj.	几个的
situation	[sɪtjʊ'eɪʃ(ə)n]	n.	情形，境遇
steep	[stiːp]	adj.	陡峭的，险峻的
street	[striːt]	n.	街，街道
tow	[təʊ]	v.	拖，曳，牵引　n. 拖
first	[fɜːst]	n.	第一　adj. 第一的
second	['sekənd]	adj.	第二的　n. 秒

练习题

1. 单词或词组英汉连线

steel belt　　　　　　　　　　　　　　　　　电控无级变速器

forward clutch　　　　　　　　　　　　　　自动变速器液

sun gear　　　　　　　　　　　　　　　　　无级变速器

multi-plate　　　　　　　　　　　　　　　　液力变矩器

torque（hydrodynamic）converter　　　　　锁止离合器

lockup clutch　　　　　　　　　　　　　　　钢带

TCC（torque converter clutch）　　　　　　前进离合器

CVT（continuously variable transmission）　太阳轮

electro-continuously variable transmission　多片的

ATF（automatic transmission fluid）　　　　液力变矩器离合器

2. 汉译英

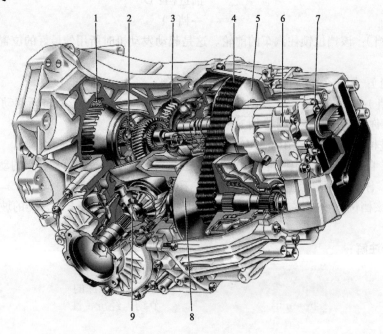

无级变速器＿＿＿＿＿＿＿＿＿＿＿＿＿＿

1—倒档离合器＿＿＿＿＿＿＿＿＿＿　2—行星齿轮机构＿＿＿＿＿＿＿＿＿＿

3—辅助减速齿轮＿＿＿＿＿＿＿＿　4—传动链＿＿＿＿＿＿＿＿＿＿＿＿

5—主动链轮＿＿＿＿＿＿＿＿＿＿＿　6—液压控制单元＿＿＿＿＿＿＿＿＿

7—电控单元＿＿＿＿＿＿＿＿＿＿＿　8—从动链轮

9—差速器＿＿＿＿＿＿＿＿＿＿＿＿

3. 英译汉

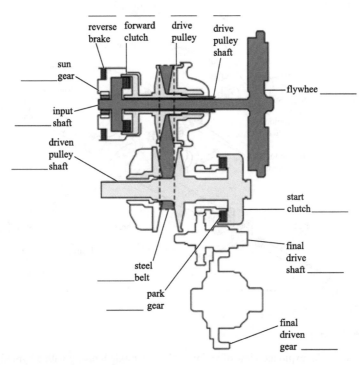

reverse brake
forward clutch
drive pulley
drive pulley shaft
sun gear
input shaft
driven pulley shaft
flywhee＿＿＿＿＿
start clutch＿＿＿＿＿
final drive shaft＿＿＿＿＿
steel belt＿＿＿＿＿
park gear＿＿＿＿＿
final driven gear＿＿＿＿＿

4. 英译汉

Dipstick

Typical location of a transmission dipstick in a transaxle.

Examples of the different ATF used in today's transmissions.

4-4 Final Drive and Differential 主减速器和差速器

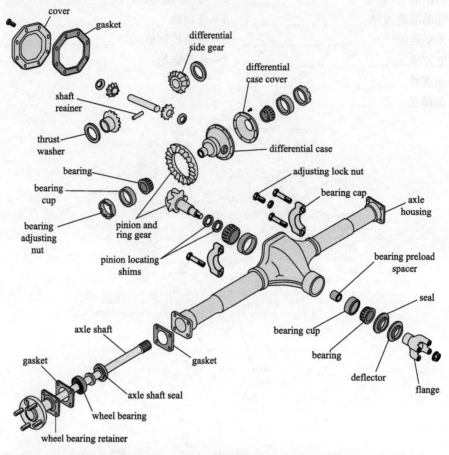

Figure 4-6 An exploded view of an integral-carrier axle housing with a hypoid final drive assembly and semifloating axles.

准双曲面主减速器和半浮式车桥的组合式桥壳的展开图

adjusting nut	调整螺母
adjusting nut lock	调整螺母锁片
axle housing	桥［轴］壳
axle Shaft	半轴
axle shaft Seal	半轴油封
bearing	轴承
bearing cap	轴承盖
bearing cup	轴承座圈
bearing preload spacer	轴承预紧隔套
cover	盖
deflector	防尘罩⊖
differential case	差速器壳盖
differential case cover	差速器壳
pinion and ring gear	小齿轮和齿圈，一套主传动齿轮
pinion locating shims	小齿轮定位垫片

⊖ "Deflector"译作"防尘罩"，是按实际用途译出。按词典则是：导流板［片］，导向装置，偏转器。

（续）

flange	法兰
gasket	衬垫
seal	油封
shaft retainer	轴锁销
side gear	半轴齿轮
thrust washer	止推垫圈
wheel bearing	车轮轴承
wheel bearing retainer	车轮轴承固定极

本课新单词

deflector	[dɪ'flektə]	*n.*	导流板［片］，导向装置，偏转器
dust	[dʌst]	*n.*	灰尘
flange	[flændʒ]	*n.*	凸缘，法兰
hypoid	['haɪpɔɪd]	*adj.*	准双曲面的
locating	[ləʊ'keɪtɪŋ]	*v.*	定位
ping	[pɪŋ]	*n.*	子弹飞过的砰砰声
planet	['plænɪt]	*n.*	行星
semifloating	[se'maɪfələʊtɪŋ]	*adj.*	半浮式（的）
shim	[ʃɪm]	*n.*	薄垫片
spacer	['speɪsə]	*n.*	隔套，隔离物

阅读材料

Why You Need a Differential

Car wheels spin at different speeds, especially when turning. Each wheel travels a different distance through the turn, and that the inside wheels travel a shorter distance than the outside wheels. Since speed is equal to the distance traveled divided by the time it takes to go that distance, the wheels that travel a shorter distance travel at a lower speed. Also note that the front wheels travel a different distance than the rear wheels.

For the non-driven wheels on your car, the front wheels on a rear-wheel drive car, the back wheels on a front-wheel drive car, this is not an issue. There is no connection between them, so they spin independently. But the driven wheels are linked together so that a single engine and transmission can turn both wheels. If your car did not have a differential, the wheels would have to be locked together, forced to spin at the same speed. This would make turning difficult and hard on your car. Or the car to be able to turn, one tire would have to slip. With modern tires and concrete roads, a great deal of force is required to make a tire slip. That force would have to be transmitted through the axle from one wheel to another, putting a heavy strain on the axle components.

Thus, a differential is necessary to solve these problems.

为什么需要差速器

汽车车轮以不同速度旋转，在转弯时更是如此。在转向时通过的距离，每个车轮行程各不相同，内侧车轮通过的行程要比外侧的车轮短。由于速度等于行驶路程与所用时间之比，行驶路程短的车轮行驶的速度就相对较低。并且，前轮和后轮行驶的距离也不尽相同。

对汽车的非驱动轮，即后驱车的前轮和前驱车的后轮而言，这并不是问题。因为非驱动轮之间没有连接，它们可独立运转。而就驱动轮而言，要使同一个发动机和变速器的动力同时传给两个车轮，这两个车轮之间就要彼此相连。如果你的车上没有差速器，两个驱动轮就必须锁为一体，迫使它们以相同的速度旋转。这将导致汽车转向困难。因为汽车转向时，其中一个车轮必须滑行。而就现代的轮胎和混凝土路面而言，需要很大的力量才能带动一个车轮滑行。这个力量必须通过车轴从一个车轮传到另一个车轮，这将会使轴组件带来大的形变。

因此，要解决上述问题，差速器必不可少。

生词短语注解：

deal	[diːl]	v.	处理，应付
distance	['dɪstəns]	n.	距离
divided	[dɪ'vaɪdɪd]	adj.	分开的
equal	['iːkwəl]	adj.	相等的
especially	[ɪ'speʃəli]	adv.	特别，尤其
forced	[fɔːst]	adj.	强制的，加压的
independently	[ˌɪndɪ'pendəntli]	adv.	独立地，自立地
issue	['ɪʃuː]	n.	问题，结果
linked	[lɪŋkt]	adj.	连接的
modern	['mɒdn]	adj.	现代的
necessary	['nesəsəri]	adj.	必要的，必需的
require	[rɪ'kwaɪə]	v.	需要，要求
slip	[slɪp]	v.	滑动，滑
solve	[sɒlv]	v.	解决
strain	[streɪn]	n.	应变，形变 v. 拉紧
turning	['tɜːnɪŋ]	n.	转向，旋转

练习题

1. 单词或词组英汉连线

deflector	车轮轴承
differential case	半轴齿轮
drive pinion	止推垫圈
flange	轴锁销
inner bearing	行星齿轮
locating shim	定位垫圈
planet pinion	法兰
shaft retainer	主动小齿轮
side gear	差速器壳
thrust washer	防尘罩
wheel bearing	内轴承

2. 英译汉

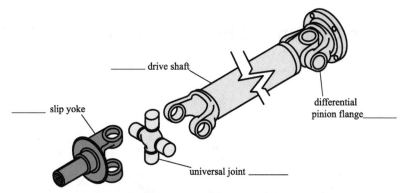

drive shaft

slip yoke

differential pinion flange

universal joint

A Drive Shaft Assembly with U-joints

3. 汉译英（写在图附近）

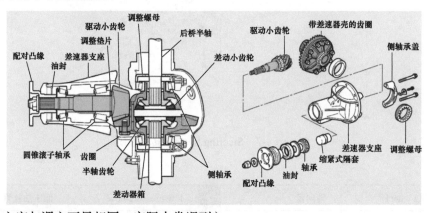

驱动小齿轮
调整螺母
后桥半轴
驱动小齿轮
带差速器壳的齿圈
配对凸缘
调整垫片
差速器支座
油封
差动小齿轮
侧轴承盖
圆锥滚子轴承
齿圈
半轴齿轮
侧轴承
差动器箱
配对凸缘
油封
轴承
缩紧式隔套
差速器支座
调整螺母

（图中文字与课文不尽相同，实际中常遇到）

注：collapsible spacer "缩紧式隔套"；pairing "配对"。

4. 汉译英

1）发动机以不同速度旋转

2）这将导致汽车起动困难

4-5 Steering System and Brake System 转向系统和制动系统

Figure 4-7 Steering System 转向系统

1	steering wheel	转向盘	7	low pressure hose	低压油软管
2	steering shaft	转向轴	8	reservoir	储液罐
3	steering（knuckle）arm	转向节臂	9	left tie rod	左横拉杆
4	suction tube	吸入管	10	right tie rod	右横拉杆
5	vane pump	叶片泵	11	power-steering gearbox	动力转向器
6	high pressure hose	高压油软管			

本课新单词（一）

knuckle	['nʌkl]	n.	关节，万向接头，（转向系统）转向节
rack	[ræk]	n.	齿条 架子
right	[raɪt]	n.	右 adj. 右边［侧］的
tie	[taɪ]	n.	拉杆 连接杆［件］，横拉撑
left	[left]	n.	左 adj. 左边［侧］的

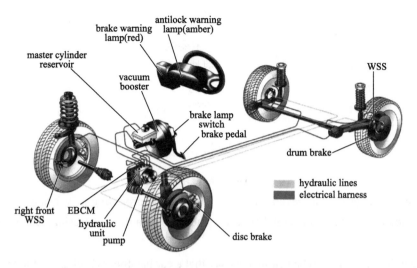

Figure 4-8   Hydraulic Brake System with ABS 带防抱制动系统的液压制动系统

ABS=antilock brake system	防抱制动系统
antilock ⊖ warning lamp（amber）	防抱制动系统警告灯
brake pedal	制动踏板
brake lamp switch	制动灯开关
brake warning lamp（red）	制动警告灯（红色）
disc brake	盘式制动器
drum brake	鼓式制动器
EBCM=electronic brake control module	制动电子控制模块
electrical harness	电气线束
hydraulic lines	液压管路
hydraulic unit ⊖	液压模块
right front WSS	右前轮速传感器
master cylinder reservoir	主缸储液罐
pump	泵
vacuum booster	真空助力器
WSS= wheel speed sensor	轮速传感器

本课新单词（二）

amber	['æmbə]	n.	黄色，黄褐色，琥珀色
anchor	['æŋkə(r)]	n.	固定件；支座（物，销）
antilock	['æntilɒk]	n.	防锁，（制动系统）防抱（死）
caliper	['kælɪpə]	n.	钳（形物），卡钳
drum	[drʌm]	n.	鼓

⊖ 这是实际中美国人在专业英语中简化运用的表现：antilock=antilock brake system。

⊖ "hydraulic unit"也常译为"液压单元"，但是此零件英语中也常用"hydraulic module"，所以可统一译为"液压模块"。

harness	['hɑ:nɪs]	*n.*	线束
master	['mɑ:stə(r)]	*adj.*	主要的
pad	[pæd]	*n.*	衬块
red	[red]	*n.*	红色 *adj.* 红色的
sleeve	[sli:v]	*n.*	套管，衬套

阅读材料

Four–Wheel Drive

Four-wheel-drive system has several different schemes for providing power to all of the wheels. The language used by the different carmakers can sometimes be a little confusing, let's clear up some terminology.

Four-wheel drive: Usually, when carmakers say that a car has four-wheel drive, they are referring to a part-time system. These systems are meant only for use in low-traction conditions, such as off-road or on snow or ice.

All-wheel drive: These systems are sometimes called full-time four-wheel drive. All-wheel-drive systems are designed to function on all types of surfaces, both on- and off-road, and most of them cannot be switched off.

四轮驱动

四轮驱动系统采用了一些独特的方案为每只车轮提供动力。不同的汽车制造商使用的措辞可能不尽相同。为了不引起混淆，我们对一些术语加以说明。

四轮驱动：汽车制造商所说的四轮驱动，通常是就短时而言，即只有在牵引力低的路况下，如非正常路面，冰、雪路面，才使用四轮驱动。

全轮驱动：这样的系统也称全时四轮驱动系统。在任何路况下，无论是正常或非正常路面，全轮驱动系统都在运行中。这一系统大多不能关闭。

生词短语注解：

cannot	['kænɒt]	*v.*	不可，不能
carmaker	['kɑ:,meɪkə]	*n.*	汽车制造商
confusing	[kən'fju:zɪŋ]	*adj.*	混乱的，模糊的
explore	[ɪk'splɔ:]	*v.*	探险，探测
full-time	[,fʊl'taɪm]	*adj.*	全部时间的，全时的
language	['læŋgwɪdʒ]	*n.*	语言，措辞
scheme	[ski:m]	*n.*	图解
terminology	[,tɜ:mɪ'nɒlədʒi]	*n.*	术语
traction	['trækʃən]	*n.*	牵引，牵引力
viscous	['vɪskəs]	*adj.*	黏（性）的
tripod	['traɪpɒd]	*n.*	三脚架；（万向节）三球销式

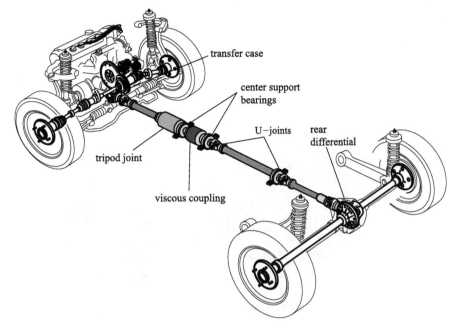

Figure 4-9 The Iayout of an AWD Vehicle Based on an FWD Vehicle
基于四轮驱动车辆的全轮驱动车辆的布置

center support bearings	中间支撑轴承
rear differential	后差速器
transfer case	分动器
tripod joint	三销式万向节
U-joints	万向节
viscous coupling	粘性联轴 [离合] 器

练习题

1. 单词或词组英汉连线

caliper	衬块
sleeve	转向节
anchor	防抱死
harness	固定件；支座销
antilock	齿条
pad	卡钳，钳形物
knuckle	线束
rack	套管，衬套
all-wheel drive	四轮驱动
four-wheel drive	全轮驱动

2. 英译汉

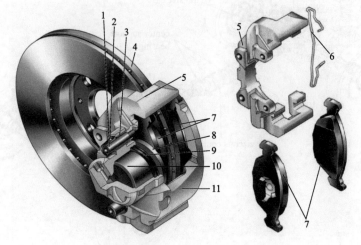

Disc Brake_____

1—bolt_____ 2—rubber sleeve_____

3—plastic sleeve_____ 4—brake disc_____

5—anchor plate_____ 6—hold spring_____

7—brake［disc］pad_____ 8—piston boot_____

9—seal_____ 10—piston_____

11—caliper housing_____

3. 英译汉

1）A reservoir cap with a fluid level sensor built in.

2）An example of a brake light switch

_____ _____

4. 英译汉

Manual rack and pinion steering gear_____

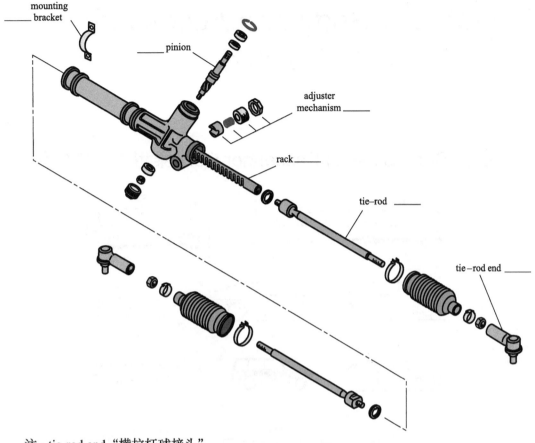

注：tie-rod end "横拉杆球接头"。

5. 汉译英

1）盘式制动器＿＿＿＿＿＿＿＿＿＿　　2）鼓式制动器＿＿＿＿＿＿＿＿＿＿＿＿

3）子午线轮胎＿＿＿＿＿＿＿＿＿＿　　4）无内胎轮胎＿＿＿＿＿＿＿＿＿＿＿＿

5）防抱制动系统＿＿＿＿＿＿＿＿＿　　6）转向系统＿＿＿＿＿＿＿＿＿＿＿＿＿

7）横拉杆＿＿＿＿＿＿＿＿＿＿＿＿　　8）支座板＿＿＿＿＿＿＿＿＿＿＿＿＿＿

9）全时四轮驱动＿＿＿＿＿＿＿＿＿　　10）短时四轮驱动＿＿＿＿＿＿＿＿＿＿

11）三销式万向节＿＿＿＿＿＿＿＿＿　　12）分动器＿＿＿＿＿＿＿＿＿＿＿＿＿

5-1 Body Class of Passenger Cars 乘用车车身分类

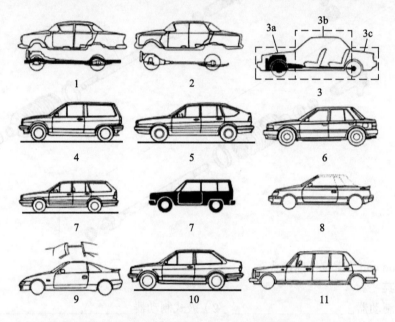

Figure 5-1   Body Class of Passenger Car 乘用车车身分类

1	full frame body，body chassis frame construction	非承载式车身
2	unit body, unitized frame（construction）	承载式车身
3	notchback body, three-box type body	折背式车身
3a	engine compartment	发动机舱［室］
3b	passenger compartment	乘客舱
3c	luggage compartment，trunk（compartment，box）	行李箱，后备箱
4	fast back body	直［快，溜］背式车身
5	hatch back body	舱背式车身
6	cut-off type body	短背式车身
	four-door sedan body	四门轿车车身
7	station wagon body，estate（wagon）body	旅行车车身
8、9	convertible（cabriolet）body, opening body	开式车身，活顶乘用车车身
9	T-bar roof body	滑顶式车身，T形顶梁车身
10	coupe body	双门（小型）乘用车车身
11	executive limousine body, pullman saloon（sedan）body	高级乘用车（轿车）车身

本课新单词

accessory	[ək'ses(ə)ri]	*n.*	附件
baggage	['bægɪdʒ]	*n.*	行李
boot	[buːt]	*n.*	行李箱
class	[klɑːs]	*n.*	种类，类别　*v.*　分类
compartment	[kəm'pɑːtmənt]	*n.*	舱，室，车厢
cut-off	[kʌt ɔf]	*n.*	断开，切开
fast	[fɑːst]	*adj.*	快速的
hatch	[hætʃ]	*n.*	（车身）两厢（式），舱［直］背（式）
luggage	['lʌgɪdʒ]	*n.*	行李
notchback	['nɒtʃbæk]	*n.*	（车身）折背式，三厢式
separate	['sepəreɪt]	*adj.*	单独的，分开的
trunk	[trʌŋk]	*n.*	（汽车尾部的）行李箱
unitized	['juːnɪtaɪzd]	*adj.*	组合［成套］的；（车身）承载式的，与车架成一体的
full	[fʊl]	*adj.*	完全的，满的
estate	[ɪ'steɪt]	*n.*	旅行车，客货两用轿车
opening	['əʊpnɪŋ]	*n.*	（开，切）口
roof	[ruːf]	*n.*	车顶，顶（盖）

阅读材料

Separate Frame Construction

In separate frame vehicles, the frame is a separate structure that runs underneath the full length of the vehicle, from the front bumper to the rear. The frame assembly is considered to be an independent part that is not welded to other body or chassis parts. The frame rests on the suspension components and wheels and absorbs the acceleration, braking and steering force, as well as the weight of the vehicle's body shell, sheet metal, bumpers and mechanical components.

The structure of the separate frame does vary, but most frames will consist of two longitudinal members or side rails made of hollow steel box or C channels. These two longitudinal members are joined at several points by steel box or C channels called crossmembers. The body shell is bolted to the frame through large rubber doughnuts or isolators to help reduce the vibration and noise in the passenger compartment.

非承载式车身

在非承载式车身结构的汽车中，车架是在整个车长下面工作的单独结构，从前保险杠到后保险杠。车架总成是不与其他车身或底盘部件焊接在一起的独立部件。车架支撑悬架部件和车轮并吸收加速、制动和转向力；同时也支撑车身壳体、金属板、保险杠和机械部件的重量。

非承载式车架结构是多样的，但是大多数的车架是由两个箱形断面钢或 C 形槽钢制成的纵梁或侧梁组成的。这两根纵梁通过被称作横梁的箱形断面钢管和 C 形槽钢在几个点上连接。车身本体通过用来减小乘客舱振动和噪声的大橡胶垫圈或隔音装置与车架连接在一起。

生词短语注解：

absorb	[əb'sɔːb]	v.	吸收
acceleration	[æk,selə'reɪʃən]	n.	加速；加速度
channel	['tʃænl]	n.	槽钢
consider	[kən'sɪdə]	v.	考虑，认为
crossmember	[krɒs'membə]	n.	横向构件，横梁
doughnut	['dəʊ,nʌt]	n.	圈，圆环形
hollow	['hɒləʊ]	adj.	空的，空心的
independent	[,ɪndɪ'pendənt]	adj.	独立的，单独的
mechanical	[mɪ'kænɪk(ə)l]	adj.	机械的
member	['membə]	n.	构件，（车身）梁
rest	[rest]	v.	依靠，支撑
rubber	['rʌbə]	n.	橡胶
underneath	[,ʌndə'niːθ]	prep.	在下面，在……的下面
vary	['veəri]	v.	改变，变化
as well as			也，同样
be bolted to			与……用螺栓安装，与……用螺栓连接
be considered to			被看作是……，被认为是……
be joined			与……连接
be made of			由……制成
be welded to			与……焊接
consist of			由……组成，包含
rest on			依靠，支撑

练习题

1. 词组和单词英汉连线

passenger compartment	单独结构
separate structure	箱形断面钢管
front bumper	乘客舱
hollow steel box	前保险杠
C channel	行李箱
convertible body	行李
accessory	机械的
mechanical	附件
baggage	活顶乘用车车身
boot	C形槽钢

2. 英译汉

Car Body Styles_____

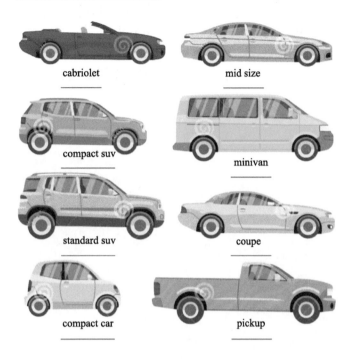

cabriolet

mid size

compact suv

minivan

standard suv

coupe

compact car

pickup

3. 英译汉

In body-over-frame construction, the frame is the vehicle's foundation.

_____

_____

Unit-body construction（sometimes called unibody）is a design that combines the body with the structure of the frame.

_____

_____

4．汉译英

1）非承载式车身_____ 2）承载式车身_____

3）箱形断面钢管_____ 4）C形槽钢_____

5）双门（小型）乘用车车身_____ 6）纵梁_____

7）车身壳体_____ 8）横梁_____

9）发动机罩_____ 10）金属板_____

5-2 Body and Terms 车身术语

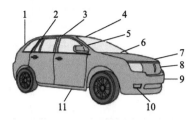

Figure 5-2 Body and Terms (1) 车身术语（一）

1	D pillar	D 柱	7	hood panel	发动机舱盖板
2	C pillar	C 柱	8	one piece grille	整体式格栅
3	B pillar	B 柱	9	soft color-keyed bumper	软色调保险杠
4	windshiele header	风窗玻璃顶梁	10	side marker ane turning lamp	侧示宽灯和转向灯
5	A pillar	A 柱	11	rocker panel	门槛（踏脚）板
6	cowl	车颈			

本课新单词（一）

color	['kʌlə(r)]	*n.*	（颜）色，色彩
header	['hedə(r)]	*n.*	头部，顶盖
keyed	[ki:d]	*adj.*	有键的，定在某调的
marker	['mɑ:kə(r)]	*n.*	标记［示，识］（物）
piece	[pi:s]	*n.*	块，片，件
pillar	['pɪlə(r)]	*n.*	柱
rocker	['rɒkə(r)]	*n.*	门槛［踏脚］
soft	[sɒft]	*adj.*	软的，柔和的
term	[tɜ:m]	*n.*	术语；期间
one piece			一件式，整体［件］

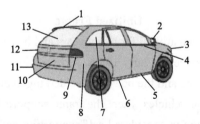

Figure 5-3 Body and Terms（2）车身术语（二）

1	rear air deflector with integrated stop lamp	集成有制动灯的后导风器
2	rear view mirror integrated with "A" pillar and side glass	集成在 A 柱和侧玻璃上的后视镜
3	front fender	前翼子板
4	belt line	腰线
5	front door	前门
6	rear door	后门

（续）

7	daylight opening	阳光口
8	quarter panel	后围侧板
9	tail lamp with stop and turn function	带制动灯和转向灯的尾灯
10	lift gate	上翻门
11	sofr color-keyed bumper	软色调保险杠
12	running tail lamp	后行驶灯
13	backlight with rear wiper	有刮水器的后窗玻璃

本课新单词（二）

backlight	['bæklaɪt]	*n.*	后窗玻璃，后窗；后灯
daylight	['deɪlaɪt]	*n.*	阳光，日光
deflector	[dɪ'flektə]	*n.*	导流板［片］，导向装置，偏转器
fender	['fendə(r)]	*n.*	翼子板（＝wing fender）；护板，挡泥板
function	['fʌŋkʃn]	*n.*	功能，作用，功能元件
gate	[geɪt]	*n.*	（车身）背门；（货厢）栏板
grill	[grɪl]	*n.*	格栅
lift	[lɪft]	*v.*	举起，提升　*n.*　举升机
line	[laɪn]	*n.*	线，线条；（电气）线路；管路
mirror	['mɪrə(r)]	*n.*	镜子，后视镜
quarter	['kwɔ:tə(r)]	*n.*	（乘用车车身的）后侧围，后围外侧板（参阅 quarter panel）
quarter panel			（车身）后围外侧板，1/4面板（指从车侧后门开口处到后灯处之间的车身面板，也有指从后轮拱到行李箱底板及车顶线之间的面板）

阅读材料

Unitized Frame

Unitized construction has been around for many years and has been commonly used by European and Japanese car manufactures since the early 1950s. Most vehicles today are of unitized frame construction. This means that the frame and the body are welded together as one structure.

Unlike separate construction vehicles where the frame supports the body and the mechanical assemblies, this type of construction is considered self-supporting and requires a high degree of body rigidity. This is obtained during the manufacturing process by pressing parts into certain shapes and then joining these components with assembly jigs and thousands of spot welds in precise locations.

承载式车身

承载式车身结构已经出现很多年了，早在20世纪50年代就被欧洲和日本的汽车制造商普遍使用。现在，大多数车辆是承载式车身结构。这就意味着车架和车身作为一个整体结构被焊接在一起。

　　不像由车架支撑车身和机械总成的独立车架构造的车辆，这种类型的车身结构被认为是车身自行支撑的，因此需要一个高硬度的车身。这种车身在制造过程中通过把零部件压制成特定的形状，然后用成千上万的焊接点和装配架将特定部位连接在一起，来获得高硬度的车身。

生词短语注解：

additional	[ə'dɪʃənl]	*adj.*	另外的，其他的
degree	[dɪ'griː]	*n.*	度，程度
enough	[ɪ'nʌf]	*adj.*	足够的，充足的，
European	[ˌjʊərə'pɪən]	*adj.*	欧洲的　*n.*　欧洲人
Japanese	[ˌdʒæpə'niːz]	*adj.*	日本的　*n.*　日本人
jig	[dʒɪg]	*n.*	夹具，装配架
obtain	[əb'teɪn]	*v.*	获得，得到
press	[pres]	*v.*	压，压制
process	['prəʊses]	*n.*	过程
rigidity	[rɪ'dʒɪdɪti]	*n.*	刚性，硬度
spot	[spɒt]	*n.*	斑点，污点
structural	['strʌktʃərəl]	*adj.*	结构的
sturdiness	['stɜːdɪnəs]	*n.*	坚固，坚固性

练习题

1. **词组和单词英汉连线**

hood	后围侧板
left fender	后窗玻璃
left front door	风窗玻璃
left front fender	行李箱盖
front bumper	格栅
grill	发动机舱盖
quarter panel	左翼子板
trunk lid	左前门
windshield glass	左前翼子板
backlight	前保险杠

2. 英译汉

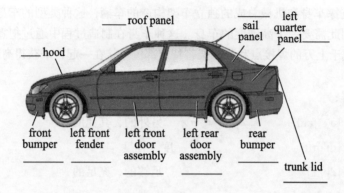

roof panel ____
hood ____
sail panel ____
left quarter panel ____
front bumper ____
left front fender ____
left front door assembly ____
left rear door assembly ____
rear bumper ____
trunk lid ____

Major Outer Body Panels

注：sail panel "导风板"。

3. 汉译英

1) 翼子板_____ 2) 前保险杠_____

3) 散热器格栅_____ 4) 发动机舱盖_____

5) 门总成_____ 6) 左前门_____

7) 外侧板_____ 8) 后围板_____

9) 行李箱盖_____ 10) 风窗玻璃_____

4. 英译汉

Chrome Exterior Accessories_____

1) 6PC. chrome pillar posts_____；

2) 4PC. chrome window sills_____；

3) 4PC. chrome molding trim_____

注：PC=piece "块，片，件"；window "车窗，（窗）玻璃"。

5-3　Supplemental Restraint System (SRS) and Seats
辅助约束系统和座椅

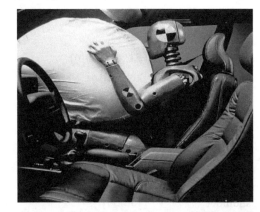

Figure 5-4　A Driver's Air Bag 驾驶员安全气囊　　　Figure 5-5　A Passenger Air Bag 乘员安全气囊

Different manufacturers also call their air bag systems by different names, such as supplemental inflatable restraint (SIR) and supplemental restraint system (SRS).

不同的制造商对安全气囊系统有不同的名称，如辅助充气约束系统和辅助约束系统。

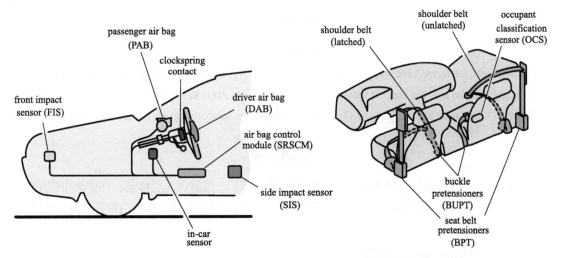

Figure 5-6　Location of Common SRS Components 普通辅助约束系统零部件布置

air bag control module（SRSCM）	安全气囊控制模块
buckle pretensioners（BUPT）	带扣预卷收器
clockspring contact	时钟弹簧接触器
driver air bag（DAB）	驾驶员安全气囊
front impact sensor（FIS）	前碰撞传感器
in-car sensor	车内传感器
occupant classification sensor（OCS）	乘客分级传感器
passenger air bag（PAB）	乘员安全气囊
seat belt pretensioners（BPT）	安全带预卷收器
shoulder belt（unlatched）	肩带（未闩好的）
shoulder belt（latched）	肩带（闩好的）
side impact sensor（SIS）	侧碰撞传感器

本课新单词

also	['ɔːlsəʊ]	*adv*	也，并且
buckle	['bʌkl]	*n.*	带扣
call	[kɔːl]	*v.*	把……叫作，称呼
classification	[ˌklæsɪfɪ'keɪʃn]	*n.*	分类，分级
clockspring	[klɒksprɪŋ]	*n.*	时钟弹簧 ⊖
common	['kɒmən]	*adj.*	普通的，通常的
contact	['kɒntækt]	*n.*	接触器，触点 *v.* 接触，联系
inflatable	[ɪn'fleɪtəbl]	*adj.*	充气的，膨胀的
latch	[lætʃ]	*v.*	碰撞，冲击
pretensioner	[prɪ'tenʃnə]	*n.*	预卷收器
shoulder	['ʃəʊldə]	*n.*	肩，肩部
such as			像……这种的，例如
supplemental	[ˌsʌplɪ'mentl]	*adj.*	辅助，补充的，附加的
unlatched	[ʌn'lætʃt]	*adj.*	未闩好的

阅读材料

Power Seats

Many vehicles today have power seats that move the front seats upward, downward, forward, and backward. Many vehicles also use support mats within the seat to fit its shape to the driver or passengers. The following Figure5-7 shows the internal parts of a typical power seat. The lumbar supports are also shown.

电动座椅

目前，许多汽车前排座椅为电动座椅可以向上、向下、向前、向后移动。许多汽车也用座椅内的支撑垫使其形状适合驾驶员或乘客。图 5-7 所示展示了典型电动座椅的内部零部件以及腰靠。

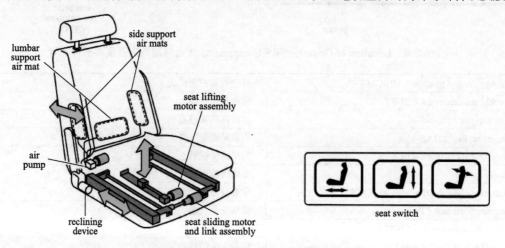

Figure 5-7　A Power Seat 电动座椅

⊖ 本处是指像时钟弹簧一样的电缆。

air pump	空气泵
lumbar support air mat	腰靠空气垫
reclining device	椅背倾斜装置
seat lifting motor assembly	座椅举升电动机总成
seat sliding motor and link assembly	座椅滑动电动机和连杆总成
seat switch	座椅开关
side support air mats	侧靠空气垫

生词短语注解：

backward	['bækwəd]	adj. 向后的
downward	['daʊnwəd]	adj. 向下的
forward	['fɔːwəd]	adj. 前进的
lift	[lɪft]	v. 举起，升起
link	[lɪŋk]	n. 连杆
lumbar	['lʌmbə]	n. 腰 adj. 腰部的
many	['meni]	adj. 多数；许多的
move	[muːv]	v. 移动
parts	[pɑːts]	n. 零件，部件
recline	[rɪ'klaɪn]	v. 使……倾斜
slid	[slɪd]	v. 滑动
support	[sə'pɔːt]	v. 支持，支撑
typical	['tɪpɪk(ə)l]	adj. 典型的
upward	['ʌpwəd]	adj. 向上的

练习题

1. **词组和单词英汉连线**

driver's air bag	闩好的
passenger air bag	碰撞传感器
buckle	电动座椅驾
seat belt	辅助约束系统
pretensioner	安全带
shoulder belt	肩带
latched	预卷收器
impact sensor	带扣
SRS	乘员安全气囊
power seat	驾驶员安全气囊

2. 短句英译汉

1）All late-model vehicles have a driver-side and a passenger side air bag.

_____

2）Most late-model vehicles have side impact, knee, and curtain air bags as well.

_____

3）The seat belt buckle switch detects whether or not the seat belt is fastened.

_____

4）The electrical circuit of an air bag system includes impact sensors and an electronic control module.

_____

3. 汉译英

1）安全气囊_____　　2）未闩好的安全带_____

3）预卷收器_____　　4）紧急锁止式卷收器_____

5）带扣_____　　6）肩带_____

7）腰带_____　　8）前碰撞传感器_____

4. 英译汉

1）Baby seat —A special designed seating device to hold safely very young children（usually under the weight of 10 kilograms）.

_____

2）Seat belts_____

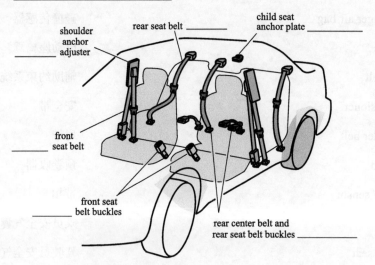

5-4 Instrument Panel Cluster 组合仪表

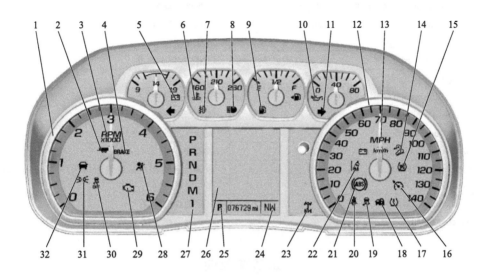

Figure 5-8 Instrument Cluster (English Shown) 组合仪表 (英制显示)

	IPC =instrument panel cluster	组合仪表
1	tachometer	转速表
2	tow/haul mode light	牵引模式指示灯
3	RPM = revolutions per minute	转每分
4	brake system warning light	制动系统警告灯
5	voltmeter gauge	电压表
	charging system light	充电系统指示灯
6	engine coolant temperature gauge	发动机冷却液温度表
7	front fog lamp light	前雾灯指示灯
8	high-beam on light	远光接通指示灯
	low fuel warning light	燃油不足警告灯
	fuel level tell-tale	燃油警报装置
9	fuel gauge	燃油表
	F=full	满
	E=empty	空
10	oil pressure gauge	机油压力表
11	turn indicator light	转向信号灯
12	speedometer	车速表
13	MPH = miles per hour	英里每小时
14	hill descent control light	下坡控制指示灯
15	traction off light	牵引力控制装置关断指示灯
16	power on / off light	动力接通 / 关断指示灯
17	tire pressure light	轮胎压力指示灯
18	security light	安全指示灯
19	traction control system（TCS）/ Stabili-Trak® light	牵引力控制系统 / 车辆稳定性控制装置指示灯（通用汽车公司自定语）

（续）

20	driver safety belt reminder light	驾驶员安全带提示灯
21	antilock brake system（ABS）warning light	防抱死制动系统警告灯
22	lane departure warning（LDW）light	车道偏移警告灯
23	four-wheel-drive light	四驱指示灯
24	NW = north-west	（当前方位）西北
25	P = park brake light	驻车制动指示灯
26	Driver Information Center（DIC）	驾驶员信息中心
27	shift position indicator（light）	档位指示灯
28	air bag readiness light	安全气囊准备就绪灯
29	malfunction indicator lamp（MIL）	故障警告灯
30	Stabilitrak® OFF light	车辆稳定性控制装置关断指示灯（Stabilitrak® 通用汽车公司自定词）
31	lamps on reminder	灯接通提醒器
32	vehicle ahead indicator	车辆向前指示灯

本课新单词

ahead	[ə'hed]	adv. 向前，在前
departure	[dɪ'pɑːtʃə]	n. 离开，偏移
descent	[dɪ'sent]	n. 下降，降落
empty	['empti]	adj. 空的
haul	[hɔːl]	v. 拖，拉，牵引　n. 拖，拉
indicator	['ɪndɪkeɪtə(r)]	n. 信号器［灯，装置］
information	[ˌɪnfə'meɪʃ(ə)n]	n. 信息，情报
lane	[leɪn]	n. 车道
malfunction	[mæl'fʌnkʃən]	n. 故障
mile	[maɪl]	n. 英里
north	[nɔːθ]	n. 北（方）adj. 向北的
readiness	['redɪnəs]	n. 准备就绪
reminder	[rɪ'maɪndə(r)]	n. 提醒器
security	[sɪ'kjʊərəti]	n. 安全，防备
shown	[ʃəʊn]	v. 显示，展出
tow	[təʊ]	v. 拖，拉，牵引　n. 拖，拉
traction	['trækʃən]	n. 牵引，牵引力
voltmeter	['vəʊltmiːtə(r)]	n. 电压计
west	[west]	n. 西（方）adj. 向西的

练习题

1. **词组和单词英汉连线**

tow/haul mode light	制动系统警告灯
camera	数字化
odometer	转速表
digital	运转，操作
stepper motor	步进电机
instrument panel cluster	组合仪表
tachometer	摄像头
operate	牵引模式指示灯里程表
RPM = revolutions per minute	里程表
brake system warning light	转每分

2. **看图短句英译汉**

1）A woofer mounted in the rear of the vehicle.

_____

2）The energy monitor for a Toyota Prius.

_____

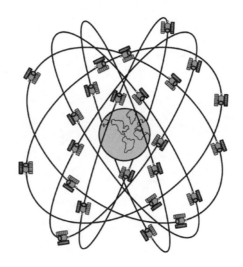

3）Global positioning systems use 24 satellites in high earth orbit whose signals are picked up by navigation systems.

_____

4）The navigation system computer then calculates the location based on the position of the satellite overhead.

_____

3. 汉译英
1）指针式车速表_____　2）车内摄像头_____

3）液晶显示器_____　4）抬头显示装置_____

5）数字化里程表_____　6）防抱死制动系统警告灯_____

7）车道偏移_____　8）四驱_____

9）西北_____　10）驻车制动指示灯_____

11）驾驶员信息中心_____

4. 英译汉
1）operate_____　2）operation_____

3）operating_____　4）GPS_____

5）reminder_____　6）ahead indicator_____

7）MPH_____　8）hill descent_____

9）reminder light_____　10）on/off light_____

5-5　Air Conditioning and Rear View Mirrors 空调和后视镜

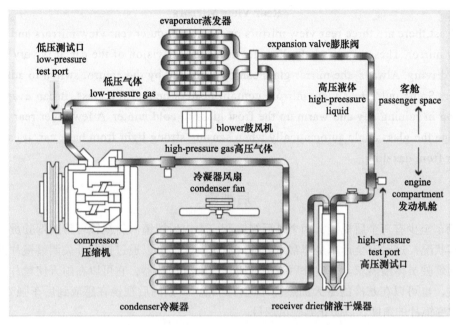

Figure 5-9　Air Conditioning System 空调系统

CCTEV=cycling clutch thermostatic expansion valve system　热力膨胀阀控制系统（这是国标规定的中文。直译是"循环离合器恒温膨胀阀系统"）

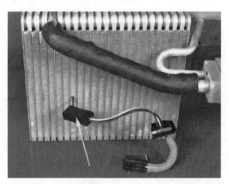

Figure 5-10　A temperature sensor mounted onto an evaporator 装在蒸发器上的温度传感器

本课新单词

blower	['bləʊə]	n. 风机，鼓风机
condenser	[kən'densə]	n. 冷凝器
cycling	['saɪklɪŋ]	n. 循环（工作），周期（改变）adj. 循环的，周期性工作的
drier	['draɪə]	n. 干燥器［剂］
evaporator	[ɪ'væpə,reɪtə]	n. 蒸发器
port	[pɔːt]	n. 口，孔，通［管］道
thermostatic	[,θɜːmə'stætɪk]	adj. 恒温的，由温控器控制的

阅读材料

Rear View Mirrors

At least,there are three rear view mirrors on a car, two outer rear view mirrors and one inner rear view mirror. These mirrors help diver to view the rear vision of the car, it is very important to safety driving. Always, the mirror glass can be regulated by the control switch to adapt different drivers.Some outer rear view mirrors contain heaters behind the glass, it can evaporate the water drop in raining day and warm up the frost glass in cold winter. A few inner rear view mirrors change the glass angle automatically when sensing strong light from back car, it can prevent the driver from dazzling.

后视镜

一辆车至少有三个后视镜，两个外后视镜和一个内后视镜。后视镜可帮助驾驶员了解车辆后方行车状况，这对安全行车是非常重要的。通常，人们可以通过控制开关调整镜片的角度以适应不同驾驶员体型需求。一些外后视镜的镜片后面有加热器，它可以在雨天使镜片上的水珠快速蒸发，也可以在寒冷的冬天加热镜片进行除霜。少数内后视镜在感应到后车强光照射时，可自动改变镜片的角度，以防止驾驶员炫目。

生词短语注解：

adapt	[ə'dæpt]	v. 适应，使……适应
automatically	[ˌɔːtə'mætɪkəli]	adv. 自动地
behind	[bɪ'haɪnd]	prep. 在……后面
change	[tʃeɪndʒ]	v. 改变
contain	[kən'teɪn]	v. 包含，包括
dazzle	['dæzl]	v. 使眩目，使眩晕
different	['dɪfrənt]	adj. 不同的
drop	[drɒp]	n. 水滴，水珠
evaporate	[ɪ'væpəreɪt]	v. 蒸发，使……蒸发
frost	[frɒst]	adj. 结霜的
glass	[glɑːs]	n. 镜片
heater	['hiːtə]	n. 加热器
important	[ɪm'pɔːtənt]	adj. 重要的
mirror	['mɪrə]	n. 镜子
prevent	[prɪ'vent]	v. 阻止，防止
sense	[sens]	n. 感觉，感应
view	[vjuː]	n. 视野，视图 v. 看，观看
vision	['vɪʒ(ə)n]	n. 景象
winter	['wɪntə]	n. 冬天
at least		至少
warm up		加热

练习题

1. 词组和单词英汉连线

warm up	后视镜
evaporator	高压
air duct	温控开关
vent	出风口
condenser	新鲜空气
fresh air	温控件
high pressure	风管 [道]
thermostat switch	冷凝器
thermostatic element	蒸发器
rear view mirror	加热

2. 汉译英

1）压缩机＿＿＿＿＿＿＿＿＿＿＿　　2）外后视镜＿＿＿＿＿＿＿＿＿＿

3）蒸发器＿＿＿＿＿＿＿＿＿＿＿　　4）风管＿＿＿＿＿＿＿＿＿＿＿＿

5）冷空气＿＿＿＿＿＿＿＿＿＿＿　　6）冷凝器＿＿＿＿＿＿＿＿＿＿＿

7）高压＿＿＿＿＿＿＿＿＿＿＿＿　　8）鼓风机＿＿＿＿＿＿＿＿＿＿＿

9）干燥器＿＿＿＿＿＿＿＿＿＿＿　　10）循环空气＿＿＿＿＿＿＿＿＿＿

3. 英译汉

1）drier＿＿＿＿＿＿＿＿＿＿＿＿　　2）glass angle＿＿＿＿＿＿＿＿＿

3）a unit＿＿＿＿＿＿＿＿＿＿＿＿　　4）blower＿＿＿＿＿＿＿＿＿＿＿

5）condenser＿＿＿＿＿＿＿＿＿＿　　6）evaporator＿＿＿＿＿＿＿＿＿

7）cycling operation＿＿＿＿＿＿＿　　8）thermostatic clutch＿＿＿＿＿＿

9）safety driving＿＿＿＿＿＿＿＿＿　　10）back car＿＿＿＿＿＿＿＿＿＿

4. 英译汉

1）Measure the temperature of the air entering the condenser.

＿＿＿＿＿＿＿＿＿＿＿＿＿＿＿＿＿

2）All sensors and switches can be checked with an ohmmeter.

＿＿＿＿＿＿＿＿＿＿＿＿＿＿＿＿＿

CHAPTER 6

Automotive Electrical and Electronic Systems
汽车电气和电子设备

6-1 Index of Automotive Electrical System 汽车电气设备索引

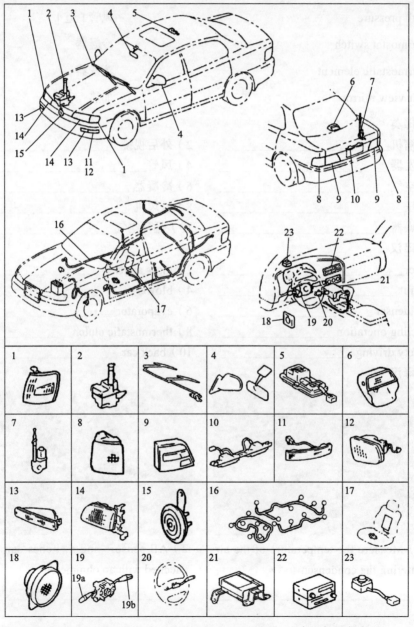

Figure 6-1 Index of Automotive Electrical System 汽车电气设备索引

1	width（-indicator）lamp, marker lamp（Light）, position lamp	示宽灯
2	windshield washer	前风窗洗涤器
3	wiper	刮水器
4	electrical mirror	电动后视镜
5	interior lamp（light）, roof lamp（light）	顶灯
6	center stop lamp（light）	中间制动灯
	high-mounted stop lamp（light）	高位制动灯
7	antenna, aerial	天线
8	back-up lamp（light）, reverse lamp	倒车灯
9	rear combination lamp（light）	后组合灯
10	license（number）-plate lamp（light）	牌照灯
11	side turn signal（indicator）lamp, lateral turn（direction）indicator	侧转向信号灯
12	fog lamp（light）	雾灯
13	front turn signal lamp	前转向信号灯
14	headlamp, headlight	前照灯
15	horn	喇叭
16	wiring	线路
	wiring（cable）harness	电线束
17	seat heater	座椅加热器
18	speaker, loudspeaker	扬声器
19	combination switch	组合开关
19a	turn signal and light control switch	转向信号和灯光控制开关
19b	wiper switch	刮水器开关
20	cruise control	巡航控制器
21	air bag ECM	安全气囊电控模块
22	radio	音响，收音机
	compact disc player	CD［光盘］播放机
23	backup camera	倒车摄像头

本课新单词

back-up，backup	['bækʌp]	*n.*	倒车
camera	['kæmərə]	*n.*	摄像头
direction	[də'rekʃn]	*n.*	方向
harness	['hɑːnɪs]	*n.*	（电）线束
index	['ɪndeks]	*n.*	索引，目录；分度
lateral	['lætərəl]	*adj.*	横向的，侧面的
license	['laɪsns]	*v.* 授权 *n.*	许可（证）；牌［执］照
loudspeaker	[ˌlaʊd'spiːkə]	*n.*	扬声器
marker	['mɑːkə]	*n.*	标记［示，识］，标志
player	['pleɪə]	*n.*	唱机，播放器
radio	['reɪdɪəʊ]	*n.*	音响；收音机，无线电
registration	[ˌredʒɪ'streɪʃn]	*n.*	登记，注册

| reverse | [rɪ'vɜːs] | n. （变速器）倒档 adj. 相反的 v. 倒车，反［逆，翻］转 |
| speaker | ['spiːkə] | n. 扬声器 |

阅读材料

Figure 6-2　A typical backup sensor display located above the rear window inside the vehicle.

典型的倒车传感器显示器位于车内后窗玻璃上方。

Figure 6-3　The small round buttons in the rear bumper are ultrasonic sensors used to sense distance to an object.

后保险杠上的小圆扣状物是超声波传感器，它用于感应与目标间的距离。

Figure 6-4　A typical fisheye-type backup camera usually located near the center on the rear of the vehicle near the license plate.

典型的鱼眼式倒车摄像头通常安装于车尾中部靠近牌照的位置。（可译为：典型的鱼眼式倒车摄像头通常位于接近车后方中间、靠近后牌照。）

生词短语注解：

fisheye	['fɪʃaɪ]	n. 鱼眼（状物）
usually	['juːʒʊəli]	adv. 通常
near	[nɪə]	adj. 近（的）
round	[raʊnd]	adj. 圆（形）的，往返的 v. 环绕
button	['bʌtn]	n. 纽扣，按钮
ultrasonic	[ˌʌltrə'sɒnɪk]	n. 超声波 adj. 超声波的
object	['ɒbdʒɪkt]	n. 目标
display	[dɪ'spleɪ]	v. 显示 n. 显示器
above	[ə'bʌv]	adj. 上面的，上述的 adv. 在上面；在……上面
inside	[ˌɪn'saɪd]	n. 内部 adj. 内部的

练习题

1. 词组和单词英汉连线

ultrasonic sensor　　　　　　　　　　　　　电子设备

backup camera　　　　　　　　　　　　　　位于的

license plate　　　　　　　　　　　　　　　显示器

radio　　　　　　　　　　　　　　　　　　电气设备

roof lamp　　　　　　　　　　　　　　　　按钮

electrical system　　　　　　　　　　　　　超声波传感器

widthlamp　　　　　　　　　　　　　　　　示宽灯

button　　　　　　　　　　　　　　　　　　倒车摄像头

display　　　　　　　　　　　　　　　　　牌照

electronic system　　　　　　　　　　　　　音响

located　　　　　　　　　　　　　　　　　顶灯

2. 英译汉

1）backup sensor_____　　2）marker lamp_____

3）marker light_____　　　4）widthlamp_____

5）electronic_____　　　　6）button_____

7）sense_____　　　　　　8）small display_____

9）American wire gauge (AWG)_____　10）direct current (DC)_____

3. 汉译英

1）危险报警开关_____　　2）电动洗涤器_____

3）超声波_____　　　　　4）顶灯_____

5）电子设备_____　　　　6）转向信号灯_____

7）印制电路板_____　　　8）电动后视镜_____

9）车尾中部_____　　　　10）倒车摄像头_____

4. 英译汉

（A）　　　　　　　　　　　　　　（B）

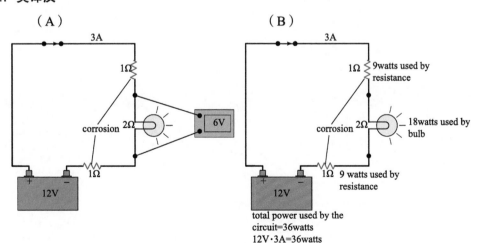

1）corrosion_____   2）9 watts used by resistance_____   3）18 watts used by bulb_____

4）total power used by the circuit = 36 watts 12V • 3A = 36 watts

5. 英译汉

1）An assortment of electronic keys and key fobs.

2）A typical start/stop button in a late-model vehicle.

3）Examples of transponder（smart）keys.

6-2   Batteries and Fuses 蓄电池和熔断器

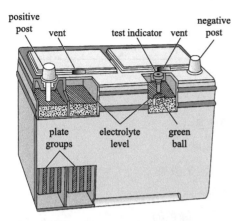

Figure 6-5   Construction of Maintenance-
Free Battery 免维护蓄电池的结构

Figure 6-6   AGM Battery 玻璃纤维吸收
垫蓄电池

AGM =absorbed glass mat	玻璃纤维吸收垫	plate groups	极板组
electrolyte level	电解液面	positive post	正极桩
green ball	绿球	test indicator	测试指示器
negative post	负极桩	vent	通气孔

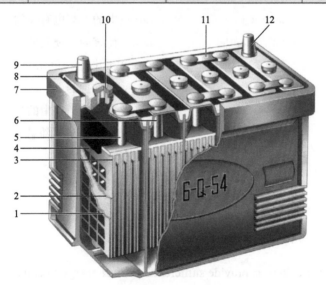

Figure 6-7   Conventional Battery 传统蓄电池

1	negative plate	负极板
2	separator	隔板
3	positive plate	正极板
4	shield	护板
5	positive plate bridge（strap）	正极板连接条
6	negative plate bridge（strap）	负极板连接条
7	case	壳
8	seal material	密封料

（续）

9	negative（terminal）post，negative terminal	负极桩（端子）
10	vent plug（cap）	通气孔塞
11	cell connecting bar（strip）	单元电池连接条
12	positive terminal post	正极桩（端子）

本课新单词

absorbed	[əb'sɔːbd]	*adj.* 吸收的
mat	[mæt]	*n.* 垫，地席
post	[pəʊst]	*n.* （蓄电池）极桩
negative	['negətɪv]	*adj.* 负的
green	[griːn]	*adj.* 绿色；绿色的
electrolyte	[ɪ'lektrəlaɪt]	*n.* 电解液
level	['levl]	*n.* 液面，水平（面，线）
test	[test]	*n.* 测试
indicator	['ɪndɪkeɪtə(r)]	*n.* 指示器
group	[gruːp]	*n.* 组
electrical	[ɪ'lektrɪkl]	*adj.* 电的，与电有关的
conventional	[kən'venʃnl]	*adj.* 传统的，惯例的
cell	[sel]	*n.* 单元电池；单元
maintenance-free	[,meɪntənənsf'riː]	*adj.* 免维护的
free	[friː]	*adj.* 免费的，自由的
maintenance	['meɪntənəns]	*n.* 维护，保养，维修
bridge	[brɪdʒ]	*n.* 桥（形物）
post	[pəʊst]	*n.* 柱，杆，桩

阅读材料

Battery

The purpose of the battery is provide sufficient electrical energy to crank the starter and operate the ignition system, computer, solenoids, lights, and other electrical components.

Batteries are made by putting together a number of cells. In its simplest form, a battery sell consists of three components: a positive plate, a negative plate, and a electrolyte（an acidic solution）.

蓄电池

蓄电池的用途是提供转动起动机，操作点火系、计算机、电磁线圈、灯具和其他电器部件所需的足够的能量。

蓄电池是由组合在一起的几个单格电池所构成的。最简单的单格电池由三个部分组成：正极板、负极板和电解液（酸溶液）。

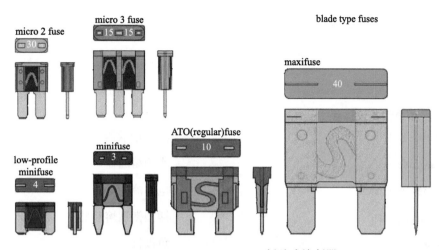

Figure 6-8　Blade-Type Fuses 插片式熔断器

micro fuse	小型熔断器（保险丝）
low-profile minifuse	矮型微型熔断器（保险丝）
mini fuse	微型熔断器（保险丝）
ATO（regular）fuse	车用（常规型）熔断器（保险丝）
maxifuse	大型熔断器（保险丝）

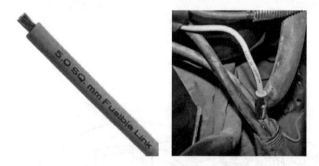

Figure 6-9　Fusible Link 易熔线

生词短语注解：

acidic	[ə'sɪdɪk]	*adj.*	酸的；酸性的
ATO=auto	['ɔːtəʊ]	*n.*	汽车
blade	[bleɪd]	*n.*	刀片，叶片，插片
electrolyte	[ɪ'lektrəlaɪt]	*n.*	电解液，电解质
energy	['enədʒi]	*n.*	能量，能
fuse	[fjuːz]	*n.*	熔断器，（俗称）保险丝
fusible	['fjuːzəbl]	*adj.*	易熔的
link	[lɪŋk]	*n.*	（链）环，连接线
low-profile	[ləʊ'prəʊfaɪl]	*adj.*	矮型的，低轮廓的
maxi	['mæksi]	*adj.*	最大的
micro	['maɪkrəʊ]	*adj.*	微（型），小
mini	['mɪni]	*adj.*	迷你型的，微型的（比"micro"更小）

| profile | ['prəʊfaɪl] | n. | 侧面；外观，轮廓 |
| solution | [sə'luːʃən] | n. | 溶液 |

练习题

1. **词组和单词英汉连线**

fusible link	测试指示器
maxifuse	小型熔断器
blade-type fuses	电解液面
positive post	矮型微型熔断器
positive plate	负极桩
electrolyte level	易熔线
test indicator	大型熔断器
micro fuse	插片式熔断器
low-profile minifuse	正极桩
negative terminal	正极板

2. **英译汉**

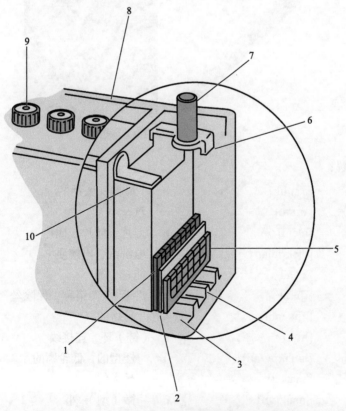

Components of a Typical Lead-Acid Storage Battery
典型的铅酸蓄电池的_____

1—positive plate（lead peroxide）_____（二氧化铅）　6—post strap _____

2—separator_____　7—terminal post _____

3—sediment chamber _____　8—case _____

4—cell rest_____　9—vent caps _____

5—negative plate（sponge lead）_____（海绵状铅）　10—connector _____

3. 英译汉

1）Battery cables connect the battery to the vehicle's electrical system.

_____

2）Normal 12-volt cable size is 2 or 4 gauge.

_____

3）The positive cable is normally red and the negative cable is black.

_____

4. 汉译英

1）铅酸蓄电池_____　2）插片式熔断器_____

3）小型熔断器_____　4）微型熔断器_____

5）常规型熔断器_____　6）易熔线_____

7）免维护蓄电池_____　8）汽车维修_____

6-3 Starting System and Charging System
起动系统和充电系统

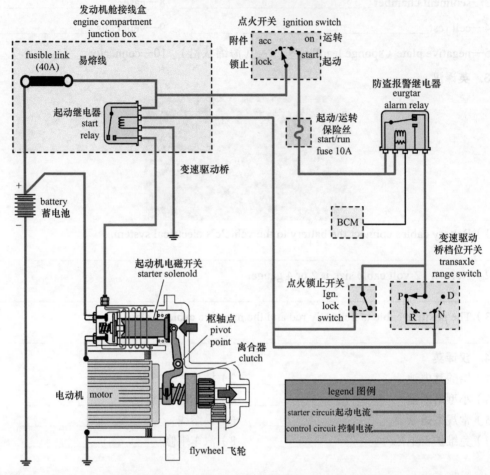

Figure 6-10　The starting system is made up of two separate systems: the starter and control systems.

起动系统由两个单独的系统组成：起动机和控制系统。

本课新单词（一）

Acc=accessory	[ək'sesəri]	n.	附件
alarm	[ə'lɑːm]	n.	警报，报警
BCM= body control module			车身控制模块
burglar	['bɜːglə(r)]	n.	窃贼
ign.= ignition	[ɪg'nɪʃn]	n.	点火
junction	['dʒʌŋkʃn]	n.	连接，接合
legend	['ledʒənd]	n.	图标符号，图例
lock	[lɒk]	n.	锁　v. 锁，锁止

made up		构成，组成
pivot	['pɪvət]	*n.* （枢）轴，支枢，旋转中心 *adj.* 枢轴的，装在枢轴上转动的
range	[reɪndʒ]	*n.* 范围，（变速器）档位
relay	['riːleɪ]	*n.* 继电器
run	[rʌn]	*v.* 运转，开动
separate	['seprət]	*adj.* 分开的，单独的

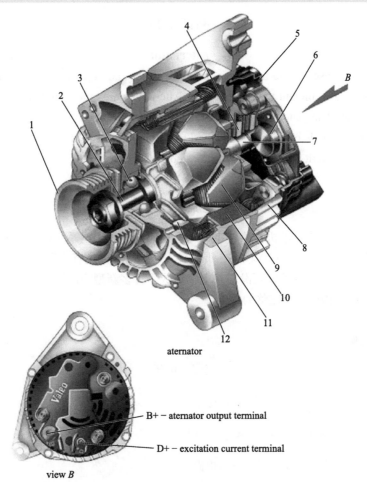

aternator

B+ – aternator output terminal

D+ – excitation current terminal

view *B*

Figure 6-11 An AC Generator 交流发电机

1	pulley	带轮	7	collector ring, commutator ring, slip ring	集电环
2	shaft	轴	8	rear end frame	后端盖
3	front bearing	前轴承	9	rotor	转子
4	brush	电刷	10	stator	定子
5	rear cover	后盖	11	drive end frame	前端盖
6	voltage regulator	电压调节器	12	fan	风扇

本课新单词（二）

AC=alternating current			交流电
alternating	['ɔ:ltəneɪtɪŋ]	v.	交替，轮流
commutator	['kɒmjʊ,teɪtə]	n.	换向器，整流子
collector	[kə'lektə]	n.	集电环［器］，换向器，整流子；收集器

阅读材料

Alternator

Today's vehicles use an alternator to charge the battery and operated the electrical circuits. The alternator is much more efficient than a generator. Alternators are much smaller, lighter in weight, and produce more current than generator.

The alternator is made of a stator, rotor and slip ring and brush assembly. Many modern alternators have the regulator built into the housings as a complete unit.

交流发电机

现代汽车都采用交流发电机，给蓄电池充电，并给汽车用电系统提供电能。交流发电机比直流发电机具有更高的效率。它体积小，重量轻，产生的电流比直流发电机大得多。

交流发电机由定子、转子以及滑环和电刷组成。许多新型交流发电机都将调节器装在发电机壳体内，与发电机构成一个完整的总成。

生词短语注解：

alternator	['ɔ:ltəneɪtə]	n.	交流发电机
brush	[brʌʃ]	n.	电刷
charge	[tʃɑ:dʒ]	v.	充电
circuit	['sɜ:kɪt]	n.	电路
complete	[kəm'pli:t]	adj.	完整的
current	['kʌrənt]	n.	电流
generator	['dʒenəreɪtə]	n.	发电机；直流发电机
much	[mʌtʃ]	adj. 许多，大量的　n. 许多，大量　adv. 非常，很
much more			更加，何况

练习题

1. **词组和单词英汉连线**

alternator   "B+" 端子

junction   电磁开关

burglar   范围，（变速器）档位

alarm   锁，锁止

relay   车身控制模块

range   交流发电机

lock   连接，接合

BCM= body control module   窃贼

solenoid   警报，报警

battery terminal   继电器

2. **英译汉和汉译英**

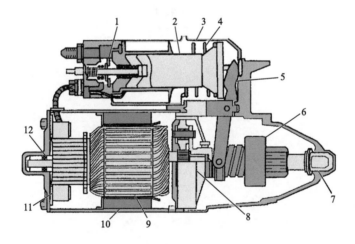

Permanent Magnet-Type Starter 永磁式＿＿＿＿＿＿＿＿＿＿

1—contact disc＿＿＿＿＿＿＿＿   2—plunger＿＿＿＿＿＿＿＿＿＿＿＿＿＿＿

3—＿＿＿＿＿＿＿＿＿电磁开关   4—return spring＿＿＿＿＿＿＿＿＿＿＿

5—＿＿＿＿＿＿＿＿＿＿拨叉   6—drive assembly＿＿＿＿＿＿＿＿＿＿＿

7—＿＿＿＿＿＿＿＿＿滚针轴承   8—planetary gear reduction assembly＿＿＿＿

9—＿＿＿＿＿＿＿＿＿＿电枢   10— permanent magnet＿＿＿＿＿＿＿＿

11— brush＿＿＿＿＿＿＿＿＿＿   12—＿＿＿＿＿＿＿＿＿＿＿＿＿＿滚珠轴承

3. 英译汉

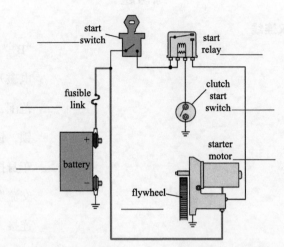

The clutch pedal must be fully depressed to close the clutch switch and complete the control circuit._____

4. 汉译英

1）前轴承_____ 2）电刷_____

3）端盖_____ 4）电压调节器_____

5）接线盒_____ 6）集电环_____

7）易熔线_____ 8）转子_____

9）交流电_____ 10）定子_____

6-4 Lighting System照明系统

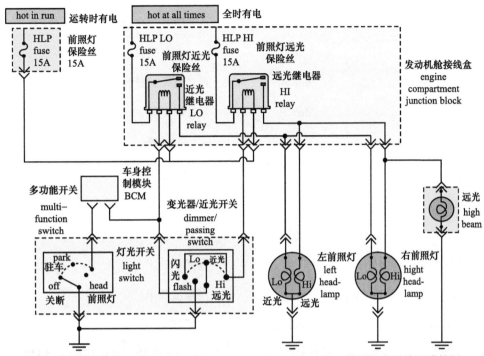

Figure 6-12 A Schematic of a Headlight Circuit With Switches 前照灯及开关电路简图

Figure 6-13 LED Lamps Used for Low and High Beams 近光和远光用的发光二极管灯

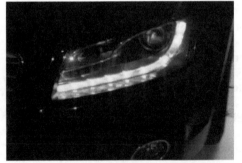

Figure 6-14 LED DRLs 发光二极管日间行车灯

Figure 6-15 A Headlamp Assembly with Cylindrical Bulb Housings 圆柱形灯泡壳式前照灯总成

Figure 6-16 A Headlight Assembly of HID Bulbs and LEDs 带高强度放电灯泡和发光二极管的前照灯总成

本课新单词

all	[ɔːl]	n.	所有，全部 *adj.* 所有的，全部的
beam	[biːm]	n.	束，光束
daytime	['deɪtaɪm]	n.	白天，日间
dimmer	['dɪmə]	n.	调光器，（前照灯）变光器
diode	['daɪəʊd]	n.	二极管
discharge	[dɪs'tʃɑːdʒ]	v.	放电
DRL=daytime running lamp			日间行车灯
flash	[flæʃ]	v.	闪光
HI=high beam			远光
HID = high-intensity discharge			高强度放电
HLP=headlamp	['hedlæmp]		前照灯
hot	[hɒt]	*adj.*	通电的，有电压的（该词通常是指"热；热的"）
hot at all times			全时通电
in run			在运转中，运转时
intensity	[ɪn'tensɪti]	n.	强度
LED=light emitting diode			发光二极管
LO=low beam			近光
multifunction	[mʌltɪ'fʌŋkʃən]	n.	多功能
passing	['pɑːsɪŋ]	*adj.*	通过的，超车的；（前照灯）近光的

阅读材料

Lamp System

To ensure that vehicles traveling at night security, and to improve its speed, the car is equipped with various lighting equipment and lighting signal devices, commonly known as the department of lights. It has become an indispensable vehicle part. According to the department of car lights installed location and different use,it can be divided into external lighting devices, internal lighting devices and automotive signal lighting devices.

照明系统

为了保证汽车夜间行驶的安全，以及提高其行驶速度，在汽车上装有多种照明设备和灯光信号装置，俗称灯系，它已成为汽车上不可缺少的一部分。汽车灯系按其安装位置和用途不同，可分为外部照明装置、内部照明装置和汽车信号照明装置。

生词短语注解：

can be			能，可从
divided	[dɪ'vaɪdɪd]	*adj.*	分开［离］的
ensure	[ɪn'ʃɔː]	*v.*	保证，担保
equip	[ɪ'kwɪp]	*v.*	装备了……的
external	[eks'tɜːnl]	*adj.*	外部的，外用的
improve	[ɪm'pruːv]	*v.*	改进，改善
lighting	['laɪtɪŋ]	*n.*	照明
night	[naɪt]	*n.*	夜 *adj.* 夜间的

练习题

1. 词组和单词英汉连线

courtesy light	踏步灯，门控灯
vanity lamp	梳妆灯
reading lamp	阅读灯
room lamp	顶灯
luggage compartment lamp	行李箱灯
light emitting diode	发光二极管
DRL	日间行车灯
LED	发光二极管
high beam	远光
low beam	近光

2. 汉译英

1）气体放电灯＿＿＿＿＿＿＿＿＿ 2）远光＿＿＿＿＿＿＿＿＿＿＿＿＿

3）近光＿＿＿＿＿＿＿＿＿＿＿＿＿ 4）高强度放电＿＿＿＿＿＿＿＿＿＿

5）踏步灯，门控灯＿＿＿＿＿＿＿＿ 6）行李箱灯＿＿＿＿＿＿＿＿＿＿＿

7）多功能开关＿＿＿＿＿＿＿＿＿＿ 8）电路＿＿＿＿＿＿＿＿＿＿＿＿＿

9）简图＿＿＿＿＿＿＿＿＿＿＿＿＿ 10）变光器＿＿＿＿＿＿＿＿＿＿＿

3. 英译汉（含图中文字）

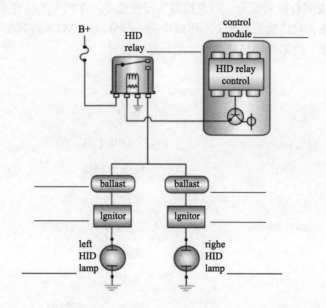

1）An HID headlamp schematic showing the lamps, ballasts, and igniters.

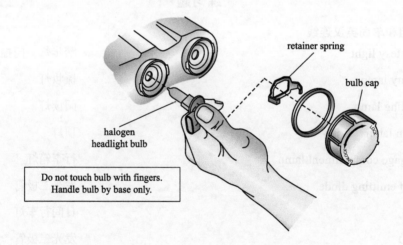

2）The correct way to install a halogen bulb into a composite headlamp.

6-5 Wiring Schematics and Symbls 电路示意图和符号

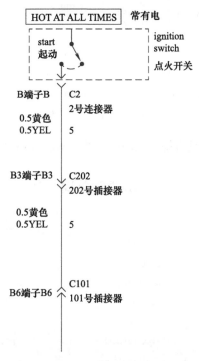

Figure 6-17　Starting at the top, the wire from the ignition switch is attached to terminal B of connector C2, the wire is 0.5 mm^2(20 gauge AWG), and is yellow. The circuit number is 5. The wire enters connector C202 at terminal B3. 从上面往下，点火开关的线连接连接器 C2 的 B 端子，该线是 0.5 mm^2（美国线规 20 号）的，并且是黄色的。该电路编号是 5。该电线接入插接器 C202 的 B3 端子。

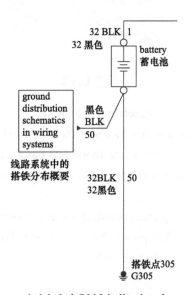

Figure 6-18　The ground for the battery is labeled G305 indicating the ground connector is located in the passenger compartment of the vehicle. The ground wire is black (BLK), the circuit number is 50, and the wire is 32 mm^2 (2 gauge AWG). 来自蓄电池搭铁点，标记为 G305，它标示搭铁插接器位于车辆的客舱内。该搭铁线是黑色的，该电路编号是 50，并且该线是 32mm^2（美国线规 2 号）的。

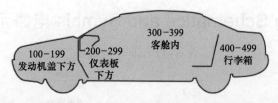

Figure 6-19 Connectors (C), grounds (G), and splices (S) are followed by a number, generally indicating the location in the vehicle. For example, G209 is a ground connection located under the dash. 各插接器 (C)、各搭铁点 (G) 和各连接处 (S) 都标示编号，通常显示在车内位置。例如，G209 是位于仪表板下方的搭铁连接。

注：电路示意图和符号还没有统一的国际标准。本项目列出的是美国标准。

本课新单词

AWG = American Wire Gage		美国线规	
American	[ə'merɪkən]	adj. 美国的	n. 美国人
attached	[ə'tætʃt]	v. 贴上，系上	
example	[ɪg'zɑːmpl]	n. 例子，实例	
labeled	['leɪbld]	adj. 标签的，标记的	
follow	['fɒləʊ]	v. 跟随，沿……行	
generally	['dʒenərəli]	adv. 通常，普遍地	
indicate	['ɪndɪkeɪt]	v. 指出 指示	
splice	[splaɪs]	n. 接头 v. 接合	
enter	['entə(r)]	v. 进入	
black	[blæk]	n. 黑色 adj. 黑色的	
BLK= black		n. 黑色 adj. 黑色的	
schematic	[skiː'mætɪk]	adj. 概要的，简［示意］图的	
YEL= yellow	['jeləʊ]	adj. 黄色（的）	

阅读材料

Electrical Schematics

Electrical schematics are used to troubleshoot the electrical circuits on vehicles. Schematics subdivide vehicle electrical systems down into individual parts and circuits. Schematics show only the parts and how electrical current flows. Schematics do not show the actual position or represent appearance of the parts.

Several numbers and identifying characteristics are also shown on schematics.The color of wire is represented by letters such as PNK（pink）, YEL（yellow）, BLU（blue）, PPL（purple）, ORN（orange）, GRY（gray）, DK GRN（dark green）, and so on.

电路示意图

电路示意图用来查找汽车上的故障。示意图把汽车电气系统细分为单独元件和电路。示意图只表示电器元件和电流流向，但不表示电器元件的真实位置或物理外观。

　　符号可以表示出一些数字和识别特征。导线的颜色用字母如 PNK（粉色）、YEL（黄色）、BLU（蓝色）、PPL（紫色）、ORN（橙色）、GRY（灰色）、DKGRN（深绿色）等表示。

生词短语注释：

and so on			等等，诸如此类
appearance	[ə'pɪərəns]	*n.*	外貌，外观
BLU =blue	[bluː]	*n.*	蓝色　*adj.* 蓝色的
characteristic	[ˌkærəktə'rɪstɪk]	*n.*	特性，特征
color	['kʌlə(r)]	*n.*	颜色
dark	[dɑːk]	*adj.*	暗的，深色的
DK GRN=dark green			深绿色
gray= grey	[greɪ]	*n.*	灰色　*adj.* 灰色的
green	[griːn]	*n.*	绿色　*adj.* 绿色的
GRY=gray	[greɪ]	*n.*	灰色　*adj.* 灰色的
identify	[aɪ'dentɪfaɪ]	*v.*	识别，鉴定
individual	[ˌɪndɪ'vɪdjʊə]	*n.*	个体　*adj.* 个别的，单独的
ORN=orange	['ɒrɪn(d)ʒ]	*n.*	橙色　*adj.* 橙色的
PNK=pink	[pɪŋk]	*n.*	粉红色　*adj.* 粉红色的
PPL=purple	['pɜːpl]	*n.*	紫色　*adj.* 紫色的
represent	[reprɪ'zent]	*v.*	代表，表现，象征
schematic	[skiː'mætɪk]	*n.*	图表，（尤指）电路原理图
several	['sevrəl]	*adj.*	几个；各自［别］的；不同的
subdivide	[ˌsʌbdɪ'vaɪd]	*v.*	再分，细分
troubleshoot	['trʌbəlʃuːt']	*n.*	故障

练习题

1. 词组和单词英汉连线

DK BLU	接头
DK BRN	指出，指示
DK GRN	电源
DK BLU	橙［橘黄］色（的）
STOP LIGHTS	简［示意］图的
HIGH LEVEL	倒车
back-up	高位
schematic	深黑色（的）
orange	深棕色（的）
power	深绿色（的）
indicating	深黑色（的）
splice	制动灯

2. 英译汉

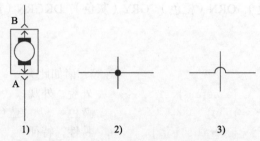

1）The electrical terminals are usually labeled with a letter or number.

_____

2）Two wires that cross at the dot indicate that the two are electrically connected.

_____

3）Wires not electronically connected

_____

3. 汉译英

1）深绿色_____ 2）浅蓝色_____

3）紫色_____ 4）浅黄色_____

5）搭铁_____ 6）符号_____

7）腐蚀_____ 8）常有电_____

9）未使用_____ 10）制动踏板踏下_____

4. 英译汉

┼	Positive	⊤	Temperatrue switch
—	Negative	▷ǀ	Diode
‖ǀ	Ground	▷ǀ	Zener diode
∿	Fuse	⊏○⊐	Motor
⌒	Circuit breaker	→C101	Connector 101
→ǀ	Condenser	→	Male connector
Ω	Ohms	≻	Female connector
⌁	Fixed value resistor	—●	Splice
⌁	Variable resistor	S101	Splice number

Electrical symbols used on wiring diagrams.

_____

Hand Tools and Shop Equipment
手工具和车间设备

7-1 Threaded Fasteners 螺纹紧固件

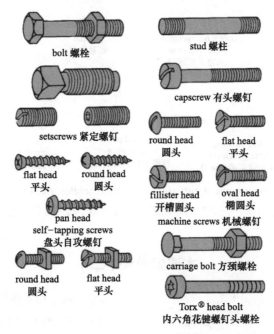

bolt 螺栓

stud 螺柱

capscrew 有头螺钉

setscrews 紧定螺钉

round head 圆头   flat head 平头

flat head 平头   round head 圆头

fillister head 开槽圆头   oval head 椭圆头

pan head
self−tapping screws
盘头自攻螺钉

machine screws 机械螺钉

round head 圆头   flat head 平头

carriage bolt 方颈螺栓

Torx® head bolt
内六角花键螺钉头螺栓

Figure 7-1　Common Automotive Threaded Fasteners 通用型车用螺纹紧固件○

　　Threaded fasteners include bolts, nuts, screws, and similar items that allow for easy removal and installation of parts. 螺纹紧固件包括螺栓、螺母、螺钉和用于零件拆装的类似东西。

本课新单词（一）

carriage	['kærɪdʒ]	n.	底座，承重装置
fastener	['fɑːsnə(r)]	n.	紧固件［物］
fillister	['fɪlɪstə]	n.	凹槽
flat	[flæt]	adj.	平（坦）的
machine	[mə'ʃiːn]	n.	机器，机械；以机器制造
oval	['əʊvl]	adj.	椭圆形的，卵形的　椭圆，卵形
round	[raʊnd]	adj.	圆（形）的　n. 一圈［周，回］

○ 参考 GB/T 3099.1—2008 紧固件术语 螺纹紧固件、销及垫圈。

self-tapping	[ˌselfˈtæpɪŋ]	*adj.*	自攻的
set	[set]	*v.*	紧定，定位
similar	[ˈsɪmələ(r)]	*adj.*	相似的，类似的
size	[saɪz]	*n.*	尺寸，大小
thread	[θred]	*n.*	螺纹
threaded	[ˈθredɪd]	*adj.*	（切有）螺纹的
Torx® head			内六角花键螺钉头

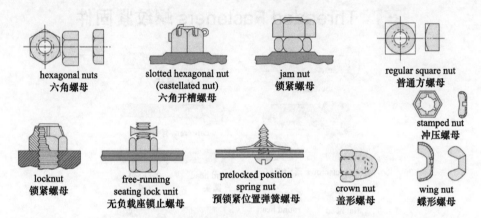

Figure 7-2　Many different types of nuts are used on automobiles. Each type has a specific purpose.
有许多不同类型的车用螺母。每种类型有一专门用途。

本课新单词（二）

arched	[ɑːtʃt]	*adj.*	拱［弓］形的
castellated	[ˈkæstəleɪtɪd]	*adj.*	开槽的，如城墙形的
crown	[kraʊn]	*n.*	盖，帽
formed	[ˈfɔːmd]	*adj.*	成形的
free-running	[ˌfriːˈrʌnɪŋ]	*adj.*	无负载的，自由运转的
hexagonal	[heksˈægənl]	*adj.*	六角（形）的，六边形的
initial	[ɪˈnɪʃl]	*adj.*	开始的，最初的
jam	[dʒæm]	*v.*	压［挤］紧，夹住
prelock	[ˈpriːlɒk]	*v.*	预锁紧
prong	[prɒŋ]	*n.*	刺，叉状物
regular	[ˈreɡjələ(r)]	*adj.*	规侧的，常规的
slotted	[ˈslɒtɪd]	*adj.*	开［有］槽的
square	[skweə(r)]	*n.* 正方形　*adj.* 正方形的	
stamp	[stæmp]	*v.*	冲压
wing	[wɪŋ]	*n.*	翼（形的），翅

阅读材料

Threaded Fasteners

Most of the threaded fasteners used on vehicles are cap screws. They are called cap screws when they are threaded into a casting. Automotive service technicians usually refer to these fasteners as bolts, regardless of how they are used. In this chapter,they are called bolts. Sometimes, studs are used for threaded fasteners. A stud is a short rod with threads on both ends. Often, a stud will have coarse threads on one end and fine threads on the other end. The end of the stud with coarse threads is screwed into the casting.

螺纹紧固件

车辆上用的螺纹紧固件大多数是有头螺钉。之所以称为有头螺钉是因为螺纹拧进了机体。汽车维修技术人员对这些紧固件不管用于何处通称为螺栓。在这一章，我们称它们为螺栓。有时我们还会用到螺柱作螺纹紧固件。螺柱是一根两头有螺纹的短圆棒。通常双头螺柱的一头是粗牙螺纹，另一头则是细牙螺纹。双头螺栓的粗牙是用于拧进机体的。

生词短语注解：

often	[ˈɒfn]	adv.	时常，常常
coarse	[kɔːs]	adj.	粗的，粗糙的
fine	[faɪn]	adj.	精细的，细（牙）的
screwed	[skruː]	v.	用螺钉固定
both	[bəʊθ]	adj.	两者的，双方的
casting	[ˈkɑːstɪŋ]	n.	铸件，铸造
chapter	[tʃæptə]	n.	章，篇
regardless of how they are used			不管用于何处

练习题

1. **词组和单词英汉连线**

spring nut	内六角花键螺钉头
crown nut	平头
wing nut	自攻螺钉
stamped nut	开槽圆头
locknut	紧定螺钉
wrench size	圆头
set screws	定位螺钉，弹簧螺母
round head	盖形［帽式］螺母
flat head	翼［蝶］形螺母
fillister head	冲压螺母
self-tapping screw	锁紧螺母
Torx® head	扳手尺寸

2. 英译汉

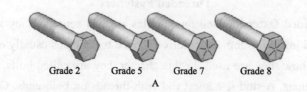

Grade 2 Grade 5 Grade 7 Grade 8

A

4.6 4.8 5.8 8.8 9.8 10.9

B

Bolt grade markings.＿＿＿＿＿＿＿＿＿＿＿＿＿＿＿＿＿＿＿＿＿＿＿＿

（A）Customary（inch）bolts—identification marks correspond to bolt strength—increasing numbers represent increasing strength.

＿＿＿＿＿＿＿＿＿＿＿＿＿＿＿＿＿＿＿＿＿＿＿＿＿＿＿＿＿＿＿＿

（B）Metric bolts—identification class numbers correspond to bolt strength—increasing numbers represent increasing strength.

＿＿＿＿＿＿＿＿＿＿＿＿＿＿＿＿＿＿＿＿＿＿＿＿＿＿＿＿＿＿＿＿

3. 汉译英

1）帽式螺母＿＿＿＿＿＿＿＿＿＿＿＿ 2）蝶形螺母＿＿＿＿＿＿＿＿＿＿＿＿

3）冲压螺母＿＿＿＿＿＿＿＿＿＿＿＿ 4）锁紧螺母＿＿＿＿＿＿＿＿＿＿＿＿

5）六角螺母＿＿＿＿＿＿＿＿＿＿＿＿ 6）开槽螺母＿＿＿＿＿＿＿＿＿＿＿＿

7）方螺母＿＿＿＿＿＿＿＿＿＿＿＿＿ 8）机器＿＿＿＿＿＿＿＿＿＿＿＿＿

9）大小＿＿＿＿＿＿＿＿＿＿＿＿＿＿ 10）自攻螺钉＿＿＿＿＿＿＿＿＿＿＿

11）螺钉头＿＿＿＿＿＿＿＿＿＿＿＿＿ 12）圆头＿＿＿＿＿＿＿＿＿＿＿＿＿

4. 汉译英 / 英译汉

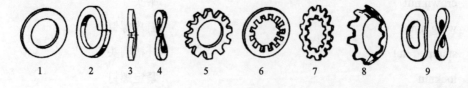

1 2 3 4 5 6 7 8 9

1）flat＿＿＿＿＿＿＿＿＿＿＿＿＿＿＿＿＿＿ 2）＿＿＿＿＿＿＿＿＿＿＿弹簧垫圈

3）curved spring washer＿＿＿＿＿＿＿＿ 4）wave spring washer＿＿＿＿＿＿＿＿

5）external tooth lock washer＿＿＿＿＿＿ 6）internal tooth lock washer＿＿＿＿＿＿

7）external-internal（tooth）lock washer＿＿＿＿＿＿＿＿＿＿＿＿＿＿＿＿＿＿＿

8）countersunk external toothed lock washer 锥形＿＿＿＿＿＿＿＿＿＿＿＿＿＿＿

9）wave＿＿＿＿＿＿＿＿＿＿＿波形垫圈

5. Torx® 中 ® 是什么意思？

7-2 Wrenches and Pliers 扳手和手钳

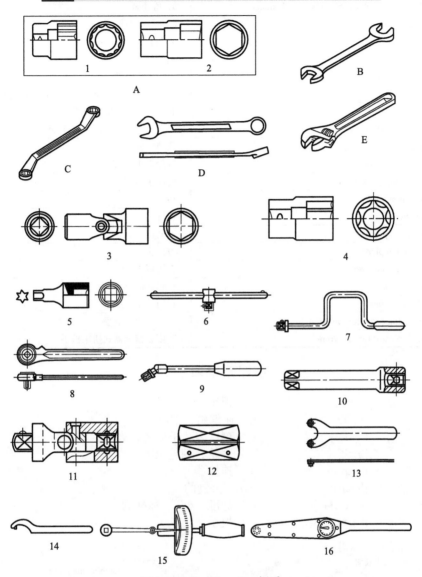

Figure 7-3   Wrenches 扳手

	Spanner	扳手
	socket	套筒
	S.A.E STD. socket	英制套筒，美国汽车工程学会标准套筒
A	S. A. E = Society of Automotive Engineers	（美）汽车工程学会
	STD = standard	标准
	Metric STD. socket	公制套筒
B	open end wrench[spanner]	呆扳手
	double open end wrench	双头呆扳手
C	box end wrench	梅花扳手
D	combination wrench	两用扳手
E	adjustable wrench[spanner]	活扳手

（续）

1	12-point socket, double-hexagonal socket	12 角套筒
	standard socket	（普通）套筒
2	6-point socket, hexagonal open type socket	六角套筒
	deep（-well）socket	高套筒
3	swivel socket, Joint socket	万向节型套筒
4	E-type Torx wrench	E 形内六花键螺栓扳手，E 形 Torx 螺栓扳手
5	T-type Torx wrench	T 形内六花键螺栓扳手，T 形 Torx 螺栓扳手
6	sliding T-handle	滑行头手柄，滑动 T 形手柄
7	speed brace[handle]	快速摇柄
8	ratchet（handle）	棘轮扳手
9	nut spinner, flex head	转向手柄
10	extension bar	接杆
	bar extension	接杆
11	universal joint	万向接头
12	square coupler	方接头
13	pin type face wrench	双销扳手
14	pin wrench	柱销钩形扳手
15~16	torque wrench	扭力［矩］扳手
15	deflecting beam torque wrench	指示式扭矩扳手
16	dial indicator torque wrench	刻度表指示器式扭矩扳手

本课新单词（一）

wrench	[rentʃ]	n.	扳手
deflect	[dɪ'flekt]	v.	使偏斜，偏斜
dial	['daɪəl]	n.	刻度表，千分表，表盘，刻［标］度盘
ratchet	['rætʃɪt]	n.	棘轮；棘轮扳手
coupler	['kʌplə]	n.	连接器
metric	['metrɪk]	adj.	公制的
standard	['stændəd]	n. 标准 adj. 标准的	
spanner	['spænə(r)]	n.	扳手

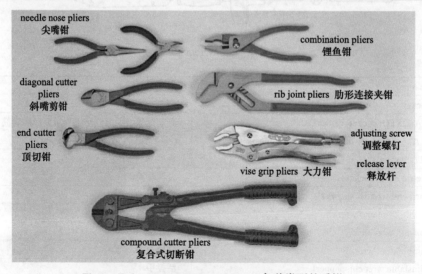

Figure 7-4　Various Types of Pliers 各种类型的手钳

本课新单词（二）

compound	['kɒmpaʊnd]	*n.*	混合物 *adj.* 复［混，组］合的，合成的
cutter	['kʌtə(r)]	*n.*	刀具，切割器
pliers	['plaɪəz]	*n.*	手钳，钳子
diagonal	[daɪ'æɡənl]	*adj.*	斜（交，线）的，交叉的
nose	[nəʊz]	*n.*	（人体）鼻，（汽车）头部；斜头形物
combination	[ˌkɒmbɪ'neɪʃn]	*n.*	组合，复合
rib	[rɪb]	*n.*	肋，肋条，加厚部
vise	[vaɪs]	*n.*	（台）虎钳
grip	[ɡrɪp]	*v.*	抓（牢），（紧）握，（紧）夹
needle	['niːdl]	*n.*	针状物

阅读材料

Wrenches

Wrenches are the most used hand tool by service technicians. Most wrenches are constructed of forged alloy steel, usually chrome-vanadium steel. After the wrench is formed, it is hardened, tempered to reduce brittleness, and then chrome plated. Wrenches are available in both fractional and metric sizes.

阅读材料

扳手

扳手是维修技术人员最常用的手用工具。大多数的扳手是用合金钢煅造而成，一般是用铬矾钢。扳手锻造成型后材料变硬，还需要回火来降低它的脆性，然后进行镀铬处理。扳手有用分数尺寸⊖和公制尺寸。

生词短语注解：

available	[ə'veɪləbl]	*adj.*	可用的，可购得的
brittleness	['brɪtlnəs]	*n.*	脆性，易碎性
chrome	[krəʊm]	*n.*	铬，Cr（= chromium）；镀铬
chrome-vanadium		*adj.*	铬钒的
vanadium	[və'neɪdɪəm]	*n.*	钒
forged	['fɔːdʒd]	*adj.*	锻造的
fractional	['frækʃənl]	*adj.*	分［小］数的，用分数表示的
hardened	['hɑːdnd]	*adj.*	变硬（的），（金属）淬火［硬］的
plated	['pleɪtɪd]	*adj.*	电镀的，覆以金属膜的
tempered	['tempəd]	*adj.*	经过回火（处理）的，回火的

⊖ 指英制，如 9/16，1/2 等。——编者注

练习题

1. 词组和单词英汉连线

adjusting screw   套筒

combination pliers   呆扳手

compound cutter pliers   双头呆扳手

diagonal cutter pliers   活扳手

end cutter pliers   两用扳手

needle nose pliers   梅花扳手

socket   尖嘴钳

open end wrench[spanner]   顶切钳

double open end wrench   斜嘴剪钳

box end wrench   复合式切断钳

combination wrench   鲤鱼钳

adjustable wrench[spanner]   调整螺钉

2. 英译汉

flat nose pliers
_____

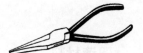

needle nose pliers
_____

multigroove adjustable pliers
_____

linesman's pliers
_____

snap-ring pliers
_____

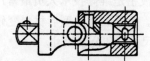

universal joint
_____

3. 汉译英

1）肋形连接夹钳_____　2）大力钳_____

3）尖嘴钳_____　4）扭力［矩］扳手_____

5）内六花键螺栓扳手_____　6）活扳手_____

7）梅花扳手_____　8）球头锤_____

4. 英译汉

tape measure
_____

stubby screwdrivers
_____

soft-faced hammer
_____

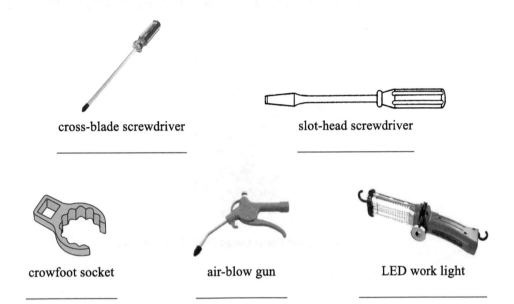

cross-blade screwdriver   slot-head screwdriver

_____   _____

crowfoot socket   air-blow gun   LED work light

_____   _____   _____

7-3 Measuring Tools and Measuring Instruments 量具和测量仪器

Figure 7-5　Typical Feeler Gauge Set 典型的成套塞尺

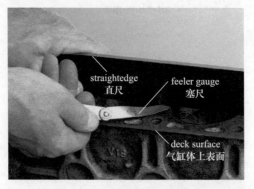

straightedge
直尺

feeler gauge
塞尺

deck surface
气缸体上表面

Figure 7-6　Using a feeler gauge and precision straightedge to check for distortion.
用塞尺和精密直尺检查挠曲。

Figure 7-7　A dial indicator with a highly adaptive holding fixture. 带高适应保持器的百分表

Figure 7-8　This dial indicator setup will measure the amount this axle can move in and out.

这样安装百分表能测量轴向总间隙。

Figure 7-9　A Digital Micrometer 数显测微计

Figure 7-10　A Vacuum Gauge Measures pressures below atmospheric pressure in units of inches of mercury.

真空表以英寸汞柱为单位测量负压（低于大气压）的压力。

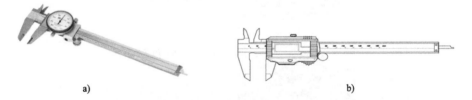

a)　　　　　　　　　　　　　　　　　b)

Figure 7-11　A vernier caliper is a measuring tool that can make inside,outside, or depth measurements.

作为量具的游标卡尺能用于内、外和深度测量。

a）Dial (Vernier) Caliper 表盘式游标卡尺　　b）Digital Vernier Caliper 数字式游标卡尺

本课新单词

adaptive	[ə'dæptɪv]	*adj.*	适合的
amount	[ə'maʊnt]	*n.* 量　*v.*	总量，合计

below	[bɪ'ləʊ]	在……下面，在……以下 *adv.* 在下面
deck	[dek]	*n.* 台［层］面，气缸体上表面
distortion	[dɪ'stɔːʃn]	*n.* 变形，扭转，挠曲
eliminate	[ɪ'lɪmɪneɪt]	*v.* 除去，消除
feeler	['fiːlə(r)]	*n.* 塞尺，厚薄规
highly	['haɪli]	*adv.* 非常，很，高
hold	[həʊld]	*v.* 把握，保持
make	[meɪk]	*n.* 制造 *v.* 做，制造；做出
micrometer	[maɪ'krɒmɪtə(r)]	*n.* 千分尺，测微计
move	[muːv]	*v.* 移动
precision	[prɪ'sɪʒn]	*n.* 精密，精确度
setup	['setʌp]	*n.* 布置，装置，建立
straightedge	['streɪtedʒ]	*n.* 直尺
vernier	['vɜːniə]	*n.* 游标（尺）

阅读材料

Measuring Instruments 测量仪器

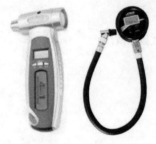

Figure 7-12　Electronic Tire Pressure Gauge
电子轮胎气压表

Figure 7-13　Non-contact Infrared Thermometer
非接触式红外温度计

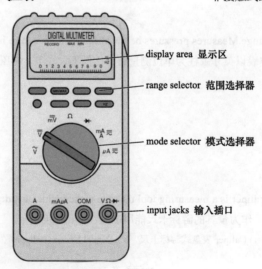

display area　显示区
range selector　范围选择器
mode selector　模式选择器
input jacks　输入插口

Figure 7-14　A digital multimeter (DMM) can measure many more things than volts, ohms, and low current. The front of a DMM normally has four distinct sections: the display area, range selector, mode selector, and jacks for the test leads. 数字式万用表能测量各种物品的电压、电阻和小电流。数字式万用表的正面通常有四个明显部分：显示区、范围选择器、模式选择器和测试线插座。

Figure 7-15　Digital Battery Tester 数字式蓄电池测试仪

Figure 7-16　Electronic Conductance Tester 电子式电导测试仪

Figure 7-17　A Battery Capacitance Tester 蓄电池容量测试仪

生词短语注解：

capacitance	[kə'pæsɪtəns]	*n.*	电容，电容量
infrared	[ˌɪnfrə'red]	*adj.*	红外线的
conductance	[kən'dʌktəns]	*n.*	传导，电导
ohm	[əʊm]	*n.*	欧姆，电阻
thing	[θɪŋ]	*n.*	物，东西，事情

normally	['nɔːməli]	*adv.*	通常地，正常地
section	['sekʃn]	*n.*	部分
jack	[dʒæk]	*n.*	插座
distinct	[dɪ'stɪŋkt]	*adj.*	明显的，清楚的
front	[frʌnt]	*n.*	前面，正面 *adj.* 前面的，正面的
thermometer	[θə'mɒmɪtə(r)]	*n.*	温度计
non-contact	['nɒnk'ɒntækt]	*adj.*	非接触的［式］

练习题

1. 词组和单词英汉连线

electronic tester	测量仪器
conductance tester	量具
deck surface	负压
dial indicator	数显测微计
thermometer	直尺
pressures below atmospheric pressure	电子式测试仪
digital micrometer	电导测试仪
straightedge	气缸体上表面
measuring tool	百分表
measuring instrument	温度计

2. 英译汉（表格中口头翻译）

Symbol	Name	Value
mV	millivolts	volts × 0.001
kV	kilovolts	volts × 1,000
mA	milliamps	amps × 0.001
μA*	microamps	amps × 0.000001
KΩ	kilo-ohms	ohms × 1,000
MΩ	megohms	ohms × 1,000,000
*Automotive technicians seldom use readings at the microamp level.		

Symbols used to define the value of a measurement on a DMM.

3. 汉译英

1）红外线测试仪_____　　2）电导测试仪_____

3）欧姆定律_____　4）万用表_____

5）轮胎气压表_____　6）成套量具_____

7）非接触式测量_____　8）毫安级_____

4. 英译汉

1）Measuring the voltage drop across the battery post and cable.

_____

2）It is easy to see why the voltage drop is high!

_____

7-4 Shop Equipment 车间设备

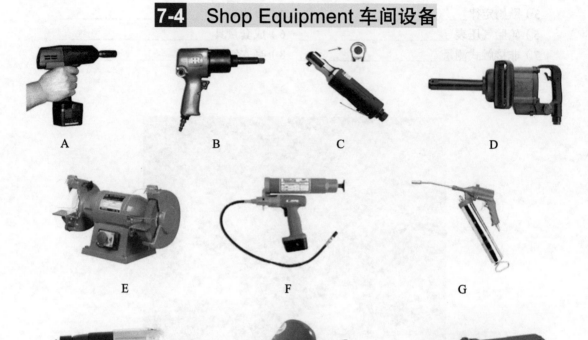

Figure 7-18　PowerTools 动力工具

A, B, C	power-operated wrench	动力扳手
A	battery-powered 3/8 in. drive impact wrench	蓄电池动力 3/8 英寸头的冲击扳手
A	electric powered wrench	电动扳手
B	impact wrench	冲击扳手
B	air impact wrench	气动冲击扳手
C	air ratchet	气动棘轮扳手
D	super duty air impact wrench	超重型气动扳手
E	bench grinder	台式砂轮机
F	battery-powered grease gun	电池供电式滑脂枪
G	air-operated grease gun	气动滑脂枪
H	air hammer	气动凿
I	dual action air sander	双动气动抛光机
J	variable speed dual action polisher	变速双动抛光机

Figure 7-19 Cylinder Boring Machine
镗缸机

Figure 7-20 A Valve Grinding Machine
气门磨光机

Figure 7-21 Wheel Balancer 车轮平衡机

Figure 7-22 Tire Changer(Changing Machine) 轮胎拆装机

Figure 7-23   A Coolant Recycling Machine 冷却液回收机

Figure 7-24   Auto-Transmission Flush Machine ATF-20DT   ATF 20DT 型自动变速器冲洗机

本课新单词

powered	['paʊəd]	adj.	有动力装置的
dual	['djuːəl]	adj.	两的，双的
gun	[gʌn]	n.	枪
polisher	['pɒlɪʃə(r)]	n.	抛光机
variable	['veərɪəbəl]	adj.	可变的，易变的
super	['suːpə(r)]	adj.	（口语）超级的，特级的
duty	['djuːti]	n.	负载，生产量
sander	['sændə]	n.	抛光机，打磨机
grinder	['graɪndə]	n.	砂轮机，磨床
grind	['graɪnd]	v.	磨削，光［研］磨
balancer	['bælənsə]	n.	平衡机［器］
boring	['bɔːrɪŋ]	v.	镗孔，钻孔　n.　镗缸
change	[tʃeɪndʒ]	v.	变化，变换，（变速器）换档
flush	[flʌʃ]	v.	冲洗
full	[ful]	adj.	充满的，满的　v.　加注

阅读材料

Shop Equipment

Some tools and equipment are supplied by the service facility and few technicians have these as part of their tool assortment. These tools are commonly used but there is no need for each technician to own them. Many shops have one or two of each.

List the common types of shop equipment and state their purpose. For example: bench vises, grease guns, presses, oxyacetylene torches...

车间设备

有些工具和设备属于维修服务设施，不在服务技术人员个人的工具分类之中。这些工具通常不归技术人员个人所有。很多车间这类工具每样也只有一两件。

这是公用型车间设备和它们的用途状况清单。例如：各种台钳、滑脂枪、压床、氧乙炔割炬……

生词短语注解：

assortment	[ə'sɔːtmənt]	*n.*	分类；种类
commonly	['kɒmənli]	*adv.*	通常地，普通地
need	[niːd]	*n.*	需要 *v.* 需要
each	[iːtʃ]	*adj.*	每［各］个（的）
few	[fjuː]	*adj.*	很少的，少数的
list	[lɪst]	*n.*	明细表，清单
own	[əʊn]	*v.*	拥有；自己的
oxyacetylene	[,ɒksɪə'setəliːn]	*adj.*	氧乙炔（的）
press	[pres]	*n.*	压（力）机，压床
supply	[sə'plaɪ]	*adj.*	提供，供给
facility	[fə'sɪləti]	*n.*	设备，装置
torch	[tɔːtʃ]	*n.*	焊［气，割］炬

练习题

1. 词组和单词英汉连线

automatic cycle   气动凿

intelligent configuration   台式砂轮机

flush machine   冲洗机

bench grinder   自动循环

battery-powered grease gun   智能化结构

air-operated grease gun   气动滑脂枪

air hammer   电动滑脂枪

2. 汉译英

1）电动冲击扳手＿＿＿＿＿＿＿＿＿＿　　2）镗缸机＿＿＿＿＿＿＿＿＿＿＿＿

3）数字式车轮平衡机＿＿＿＿＿＿＿＿　　4）冷却液交换机＿＿＿＿＿＿＿＿＿

5）智能型 ATF 液交换机＿＿＿＿＿＿　　6）进度表＿＿＿＿＿＿＿＿＿＿＿＿

7）车轮动平衡机＿＿＿＿＿＿＿＿＿＿　　8）电动抛光机＿＿＿＿＿＿＿＿＿＿

9）自动工作＿＿＿＿＿＿＿＿＿＿＿＿　　10）合理的清洁＿＿＿＿＿＿＿＿＿

3. 英译汉

1）automatic change＿＿＿＿＿＿＿＿＿　　2）easy operation＿＿＿＿＿＿＿＿＿

3）reasonable＿＿＿＿＿＿＿＿＿＿＿＿　　4）thorough recycling＿＿＿＿＿＿＿

5）battery-powered＿＿＿＿＿＿＿＿＿＿　　6）powered＿＿＿＿＿＿＿＿＿＿＿＿

7）tire changing machine＿＿＿＿＿＿＿　　8）boring machine＿＿＿＿＿＿＿＿＿

4. 英译汉

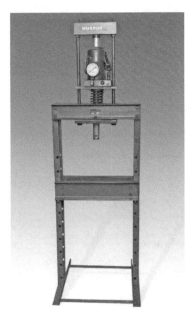

1）**A floor-mounted hydraulic press.** A hydraulic press is usually used to press bearings on and off on rear axles and transmissions.

2）**A typical vise mounted to a workbench**. A bench vise is used to hold components so that work can be performed on the unit. The size of a vise is determined by the width of the jaws.

5. 英译汉（口头翻译）

E-mail to this supplier

* From: [_____] Enter your e-mail please.

* To: **Engine Garage Enquipment Co,.Ltd**

* Subject: [Can you supply auto- transmission flush machine ATF-5800 for us?]

* Message: [   ]

Characters Remaining: (**0**/3000)

✉ **Send**

7-5　Diagnostic Testers　诊断仪

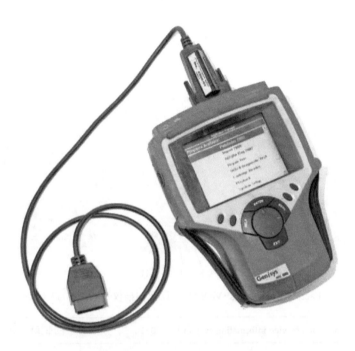

Figure 7-25　A Scan Tool 扫描仪

Figure 7-26　An Engine Analyzer 发动机分析仪

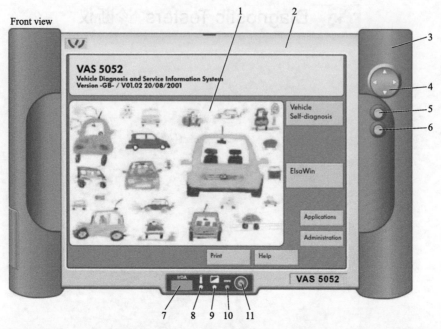

Figure 7-27　Factory Scan Tools-VAS 5052 厂家扫描仪—VAS 5052（大众 / 奥迪公司）

	vehicle diagnostic and service information system VAS5051		汽车诊断和服务信息装置
	version-GB		英文版
	vehicle self-diagnosis		汽车自诊断
	ElsoWin（源自德语）=（英语）electronic service information system		电子服务信息系统
	administration		管理
	application		使用
	print		打印
	help		帮助
	front view		前视图
1	touchscreen		触摸屏
2	system housing		装置外壳
3	rechargeable battery slot		可充电池槽
4	navigator button for mouse		鼠标导向按钮
5、6	function button		功能按钮
7	infrared		红外线的
8	excess temperature display		超温显示
9	charge status display		充电状态显示
10	external power supply display		外电源显示
11	On/Off switch		接通 / 关断开关

本课新单词

administration	[əd,mɪnɪ'streɪʃn]	n.	管理
application	[,æplɪ'keɪʃn]	n.	应［运，使］用，（计算机）应用程序
diagnostic	[,daɪəg'nɒstɪk]	adj.	诊断
excess	[ɪk'ses]	n.	超过，过度　adj.　超过的，过度的
factory	['fæktri]	n.	工厂
function	['fʌŋkʃn]	n.	功能
help	[help]	v.	帮助
infrared	[,ɪnfrə'red]	adj.	红外线的
mouse	[maʊs]	n.	鼠标（器）
navigator	['nævɪgeɪtə(r)]	n.	导航员［装置］
print	[prɪnt]	v.	打印
rechargeable	[ri:'tʃɑ:dʒəbl]	adj.	可再充电的
scan	[skæn]	v.	扫描，观［检］测
slot	[slɒt]	n.	槽，狭长孔
touchscreen	[tʌtʃɪzk'ri:n]	n.	触摸屏（=touch 触摸 +screen 屏）
version	['vɜ:ʃn]	n.	版本

阅读材料

Scan Tools

A scan tool is a microprocessor designed to communicate with the vehicle's computers. Connected to the electronic control system through diagnostic connectors, a scan tool can access diagnostic trouble codes（DTCs）, run tests to check system operations, and monitor the activity of the system. Trouble codes and test results are displayed on a screen or printed out on the scan tool's printer.

扫描仪

扫描仪是专门设计用于和车辆计算机进行通信的微处理器。扫描仪通过诊断接头与电子控制系统连接，扫描仪可读取诊断故障码（DTCs），可以对系统的工作进行测试检查并监视系统的运行情况。故障码及测试结果会在显示屏上显示还可通扫描仪的打印机打印出来。

生词短语注解：

access	['ækses]	v.	读取；进入，访问
activity	[æk'tɪvəti]	n.	动，行动；活力
communicate	[kə'mju:nikeɪt]	v.	通信；交通
computer	[kəm'pju:tə(r)]	n.	计算机，电脑
design	[dɪ'zaɪn]	v.	打算将……用作
microprocessor	[,mɒɪkrəʊ'prəʊsesə(r)]	n.	微处理器
monitor	['mɒnɪtər]	n.	监视器；监视

printer	['prɪntə]	n.	打印机
result	[rɪ'zʌlt]	n.	结果
screen	[skri:n]	n.	屏，屏幕
trouble	['trʌbl]	n.	故障

练习题

1. 词组和单词英汉连线

self-diagnosis   进入编程

select vehicle system   匹配

engine electronics   车辆自诊断

gearbox electronics   选择车辆系统

read data block   发动机电子设备

read individual measured value   变速器电子设备

adaptation   读取数据块

login procedure   读取单个测量值

factory scan tool   准备就绪

readiness   厂家扫描仪

2. 英译汉

1）diagnostic connector＿＿＿＿＿＿＿＿＿　　2）DTCs＿＿＿＿＿＿＿＿＿＿＿＿＿＿＿

3）final control diagnosis＿＿＿＿＿＿＿＿　　4）basic setting＿＿＿＿＿＿＿＿＿＿＿＿

5）fault memory＿＿＿＿＿＿＿＿＿＿＿＿　　6）end output＿＿＿＿＿＿＿＿＿＿＿＿＿

7）diagnostic trouble code＿＿＿＿＿＿＿　　8）all-wheel drive electronics＿＿＿＿＿＿

9）scan tool's printer＿＿＿＿＿＿＿＿＿　　10）factory equipment＿＿＿＿＿＿＿＿＿＿

3. 汉译英

1）服务信息＿＿＿＿＿＿＿＿＿＿＿＿＿　　2）帮助＿＿＿＿＿＿＿＿＿＿＿＿＿＿＿＿

3）计算机触摸屏＿＿＿＿＿＿＿＿＿＿＿　　4）可再充电的电池＿＿＿＿＿＿＿＿＿＿＿

5）槽，狭长孔＿＿＿＿＿＿＿＿＿＿＿＿　　6）厂家诊断仪＿＿＿＿＿＿＿＿＿＿＿＿＿

7）鼠标（器）＿＿＿＿＿＿＿＿＿＿＿＿　　8）功能＿＿＿＿＿＿＿＿＿＿＿＿＿＿＿＿

9）红外线的＿＿＿＿＿＿＿＿＿＿＿＿＿　　10）自诊断＿＿＿＿＿＿＿＿＿＿＿＿＿＿＿

11）过度的＿＿＿＿＿＿＿＿＿＿＿＿＿　　12）公制版本＿＿＿＿＿＿＿＿＿＿＿＿＿＿

4. 短句英译汉

1）A scan tool is a microprocessor designed to communicate with the vehicle's computers.

2）When performing a complete engine performance analysis, an engine analyzer can be used.

注：perform "履行，执行"。

3）Touchscreen, touching the screen replaces the function of a mouse or keypad.

注：touch "接触，触摸"。